"This book conta important and meaningful communications from the afterlife that have ever appeared in print and is as such required reading for all open-minded people in our time."

– David Lorimer, *Science, Consciousness and Ultimate Reality*

"Joanne Helfrich's book is the result of some astonishing channeling of the dead. The communications are wonderful — witty, full of insights and of wisdom. Terrific reading."

– Prof. Lance St. John Butler, Chairman of the Arthur Conan Doyle Centre

"A remarkable book... I recommend that readers keep an open mind while immersing themselves in what is easily one of the most fascinating works they will encounter."

– Stanley Krippner, Ph.D., co-author, *Personal Mythology*

"How many of us have wished for direct conversation with marvelous planetary elders no longer with us on Earth?

For me — and I hope countless others — this book so packed with their insights and wisdom in reflection after completing these lives, is that dream come true!"

– Elisabet Sahtouris, Ph.D., evolution biologist and futurist; author of *Gaia's Dance: The Story of Earth & Us*

"This book sets its own gold standard in respect of broadening our understanding of what may await us beyond this physical reality.

Moreover, the notable personalities within bring both valuable insight and practical assistance on how we can transition to the enlightened post-shift world."

– Chris W.E. Johnson MSc, author, *It's About You*

AFTERLIVES

FIRSTHAND ACCOUNTS OF TWENTY NOTABLE PEOPLE

JOANNE HELFRICH

NEWWORLDVIEW

NewWorldView
Topanga, California
newworldview.com

Joanne Helfrich
joannehelfrich.com

The Way of Spirit: Teachings of Rose
thewayofspirit.com

Cover images:
Charcompix / Shutterstock
MarShot / Shutterstock

First Printing: November 2021
ISBN: 978-0-9828123-7-2

10 9 8 7 6 5 4 3 2 1

*This book is dedicated to those
who need reminding that you are
not alone, that you are loved, and
that the world needs you in it.*

CONTENTS

FOREWORD
by Joanne Helfrich

For decades, I never considered that I might have psychic gifts. Then someone showed me what was possible: Jane Roberts (1929-1984), channeler of the Seth Material. Jane would enter an altered state and allow the Seth personality to speak through her. His words were recorded by hand and transcribed by Jane's husband, Robert Butts (1919-2008).

Today the Seth Material is considered by many to be the gold standard of the modern era of channeling for its depth, clarity, and value for personal well-being and transformation. How could I have guessed when I read the phenomenal *Seth Speaks*, in 1985, that Jane would someday write the Introduction and closing chapter for my own book dealing with afterlife communications?

Jane's psychic abilities also extended into communications with those in the afterlife, in which she "channeled" what she termed the "worldviews" of Rembrandt van Rijn (1606-1669), Paul Cézanne (1839-1906), and William James (1842-1910).[1] She didn't claim to be literally speaking with them but tuning into a kind of "energy deposit" similar to what is called the Akashic Record in esoteric circles.

Thanks to Jane's work and others who subsequently expanded its core principles, the word *channeling* (although Jane didn't like the word) has

---

[1] *The World View of Rembrandt, The World View of Paul Cézanne: A Psychic Interpretation*, and *The Afterdeath Journal of an American Philosopher: The World View of William James* by Jane Roberts.

become a mainstream term for engaging a "higher intelligence" and speaking, writing, or drawing what comes through. Channeling is also used to describe someone empathically expressing another person's energy, as actors often do.

I discovered through my education and experience that each of us has the innate ability to channel energies beyond what we may consider "our own." And because each of us has a unique *intent—our soul's innate design for our deepest fulfillment*—each expression of channeling is unique, too, resulting in wonderful works of artistry, healing, physical feats, and other natural, inspired acts.

In 2007, I discovered my ability to channel Rose who, like Seth, describes herself as an *energy personality essence*, also known as a soul or spirit. It started with my deep desire to help people connect with their soul intent. I'd never been great at using a Ouija Board but decided it might be the best way to do little readings for people. For ten days, I mostly just stared at the lifeless planchette at my fingertips. Then it started moving a little… then a little more… and finally, Rose came through! Letters turned to words, then paragraphs, then many handwritten pages.

Rose encouraged me to place my hands on my computer keyboard and intuitively move my fingers across it in a process called *autotyping*. This is generally my process to date. I go into a conscious trance state—aware but detached—and allow my fingers to intuitively move on my keyboard or in thin air (which I call *airtyping*) and ascertain the words as I engage helpful energies who write or speak through me.

Rose and I went on to write books and a website (*thewayofspirit.com*) and hold private sessions. It was in these private sessions that I discovered my ability to communicate with specific nonphysical people. Clients occasionally asked me to contact their departed loved ones, and — to my surprise — I did, but only in a limited fashion. I experimented on my own with mediumship — speaking with individuals who had passed — but my concern about authenticity prevented me from sharing the results at that time.

In 2015, I read a book about the late author J. D. Salinger, whose work I've always loved. Do you know that feeling, when you read someone's book, that they're present with you, and you don't want them to leave because you'd miss them too much? That's how I felt about Salinger, so I tried to talk with him. Our book, *The Afterlife of J.D. Salinger: A Beautiful Message from Beyond* was the result.

It wasn't until Anthony Bourdain's death in June 2018 that I tried again to speak with someone who had passed. I was so heartened by the session that I published it on my blog, and readers connected with it. More than a year later, I was inspired by an impulse to speak with Hunter S. Thompson. More conversations followed. I read each new transcript to my husband Paul, and nephew Dan, after Sunday dinners. As more personalities showed up, I considered putting their accounts into a book.

I knew from Jane's worldview journals that this was possible, but I had no idea how to do it. How would a book be organized? Who would come through? Would they all be people who had authored books? Would there be chapters, and flow between chapters, or would I have the potentially massive job of organizing them? Would their work even add up to a cohesive book? The quality of the work was so promising that I knew I had to continue and figure it out as I went along.

To help me move forward, I set a "psychic invitation" for each person to talk about their lives — physical and nonphysical — and provide advice to our readers. While most who came through were authors of published works, I began to consider them all as authors because they all wrote through me.

As such, I asked that they collaborate as a "Committee" to ensure flow and a valuable reading experience. Sometimes their accounts seemed so complete that I didn't have questions, and sometimes I did, so I included my questions and comments in italics to provide context. You'll see from these passages that I had a lot to figure out!

You may be asking as I did: how does the process work? Rose describes it as a collaboration between the authors — alive in a bardo or afterdeath state in which their personalities exist as a "blueprint" of who they were — and their own essence Self, or soul. Rose, having knowledge of each author and their essence, serves as a "traffic cop" to help translate these energies into a form I can receive. Rose might also be considered a multidimensional radio transmitter, and I the radio who tunes into each author's "station frequency." The authors' use of both "I" and "we" reflects this collaboration between who they were and who they have evolved to be in the afterlife.

This book also explores how physical and nonphysical personalities are bound together and

4

pulled apart by intent, which I described earlier as our soul's innate design for our deepest fulfillment. Intent is what colors reality creation with many kinds of expressions. Rose, the authors, and I share the intent to help bring what's needed into the world now with regard to our own lives' intents, for this continues even after we're dead.

One of the main themes across all of the accounts is that "we go as we are" into the afterlife and take our physical, mental, emotional, and spiritual challenges with us. This is consistent with Seth, Rose, and other nonphysical teachers' reports that our afterdeath experiences are influenced by our personal belief systems — which help create our reality now, too.

None of the authors report that physical death immediately ended their challenges, including the three who died by suicide. Some share the process they went through to resolve their challenges after they became nonphysical. The bottom line is, there's no better time to address our challenges and enjoy life than now, while we're physical.

The authors offer a wealth of advice, including this from George Harrison:

> We here, in our own physically nonphysical space, are here to encourage everybody ... to escape from the world's problems by tuning into their greater Selves, their Goodness, which I have tried to communicate in songs. Go listen to them again because they will help you. We here will sing them with you if you want, or sing them solo, it doesn't matter. What matters is that you feel better about everything.

It turns out that the politics of personality are real in nonphysical reality, too. I learned this through a friendly battle of wills with one of the authors (psst… it was Ayn Rand). Moreover, the global political realities of inequality and injustice of my time — evident in the events that occurred while the book was being written — call on me to say that the authors herein are not as multi-gendered and multi-hued as we need going forward. Yet, they do reflect my own heartfelt interests and concerns which attracted me to them in the first place. Every author of this book has shared profoundly helpful information, and I'm honored and grateful to include them in these pages.

The authors were also extremely helpful to me during the process and helped me cope with lingering doubts. Why were they choosing to do this with <u>me</u>? Was I doing this <u>right</u>? I understood that Rose was needed for the transmission between the individual, their essence, and me, but would that dilute the message of who they were when physical, or nonphysical? Hunter S. Thompson explained it for me:

> The reason I chose to come through you is because you have a good sense about people like me who have things to say without needing to be "whole" in the sense that you have been raised to believe. Do you follow?

> *I think so. Some people might not think of you as enlightened… or whole, as you say. They would expect Mother Teresa.*

> That's right. The part about being whole is giving you a sense of what this book is about,

too, right? So, potentially many people will need this little lesson in life besides you. Who else could reach those people? Not you, necessarily. Not Rose.

Right.

The way to view my work is through my books, primarily. I'm not going to be any different than who I was on earth. Some of this stuff has to come from Rose or this would not be the kind of book you will want to do.

Really? What would kind of book would that be, if you were to write it through me, without Rose?

It would be full of bitterness and love for people who are still alive, who I need to contact in order to feel better about myself now, which is the kind of thing that I would approve of if I had not adopted this worldview that Rose has provided through my interacting with her.

Thank you. I wouldn't want to do that book either. It wouldn't be as insightful. And every dead person would want one!

Of course, a discerning reader has to wonder, "Is it really <u>them</u>?" Well, I know it's <u>not me</u>. I remain <u>me</u> through the channeling process. I sense the energy of these personalities as my fingers move on my keyboard. I remain detached, keeping my ego self out of the way, but my identity is never threatened or diminished. In fact, this book helped me to expand how I think of my "self" and may do the same for you.

You may also be asking, "Is this book a work of fact or fiction?" Modern materialist science may never be able to prove the existence of the afterlife because its way of knowing the truth is limited to our <u>physical outer</u> sense perception and disregards what it can't prove empirically. Therefore, we also need to use <u>nonphysical inner</u> senses to further determine what's true. While this book isn't fiction, it was, like fiction, created by using outer and inner senses, as is all art, in my view.

Here, then, is the most important question for me: <u>is the book helpful</u>? As you'll discover, helpfulness is the reason for its existence, and the aim of every soul—physical and nonphysical—who created it. These nonphysical authors are also its beneficiaries, as in the words of John Barron, "Each soul needs a place to share their stories." These authors yearn to share their experiences and wisdom, and to help us in our daily lives.

In addition to the authors, I wish to thank my husband Paul for his scholarship, editing, and helping me feel safe and loved; our nephew Dan Scott (and Xylah) for his open and enthusiastic presence during this adventure; colleague Chris Johnson for keeping our work vibrant and fun; art and soul sister Barbara LeVan Fisher for guiding the cover design; and David Lorimer and Lance Butler for their gracious endorsements and for welcoming me into their communities.

I hope you'll enjoy the company of these dearly undeparted souls as much as I have!

Joanne Helfrich
Topanga, California
November 2021

INTRODUCTION
by Jane Roberts

My name is Jane Roberts. I lived in the United States from 1929 until my death in 1984. During that time, I wrote a wide variety of books—from science fiction, to poetry, to what I am best known for—the Seth Material. This material was transmitted through me by an energy personality essence who called himself Seth and transcribed by my husband Robert Butts.

The most unusual thing about this work is that while it was dictated by an entity that was not physical, it is very life affirming. That's what you will get from this book, too, because what better way to celebrate your physical lives than to allow yourself to realize that life is eternal, that you have many things to look forward to, and that there are certain habits and thoughts to help you in this life as well as beyond it?

That's what this book will help you do: release your fears about the next phase of your eternal soul while stretching your thinking in ways that are truly spectacular.

I have been spectacularly nonphysical for the many years since my physical death, always wanting to shed some light on my work with Seth, which has been received so well by many individuals who read it. The work itself has beauty to it—I know—and has magnificence to it as well. However, I'm not the author, nor have I been at any time.

The process involved an energy personality essence—Seth—who was able to construct a flow of ideas from the author in the nonphysical world to the author in the physical world. What you might think of as my oversoul—Ruburt—was involved with the transmission, too. The expertise from many lifetimes also fed the work through the experiences of both Seth and Ruburt. This was not something I took lightly. This required a great deal of energy and focus.

With the help of my Robbie, I was able to tell the world about the afterlife, about consciousness, about so many things. However, it was not necessarily mine to tell. I was the receiver and writer who had to affix my name to the books.

This was very similar to this situation in which Joanne hears my thoughts then transcribes them, all the while being helped by her own oversoul—or *essence* as we call it—and Rose, the sort of energy personality essence like Seth who serves as the overseer in the sense that I described earlier. The way I think about this role that Joanne and I found ourselves in is as an "author of authors" who has the ability to discern what's required to make something like this happen, then does so.

I can't believe I'm now the one who is helping with the transmission, being on the other side of this complex process, as I was always the one in her shoes! However, I do realize there are others who do this kind of work and I help them, too. It's something I cherish now as much as I ever did, although the roles are a bit different.

When I had the opportunity to engage with this project, I was not going to do it at first because I did not realize what was required. I had to sort through my own belief systems to see if this would be fun or beneficial for me, and I determined that it would. You do the same when you take in any information, and that's what I would like to impart to you now before you read further: be discerning. Don't take anyone's word for anything. You have the gifts of the gods in you to decide if or when you will believe what you believe.

The important thing to realize is that your beliefs are extremely important to look at. You create your reality based on your beliefs. I had the opportunity to sort through mine, then realized this was about the most fun project I have ever wanted to do!

I engage with a group of others to help sort out what she will write. She has asked for our help — the Committee of authors, as she calls us — and we help put things together for her, acting collaboratively before she even gets to the typewriter, or keyboard, as you call it these days. I also help with translations from others who have gone past their immediate afterdeath environment. Those still in their afterdeath environment are readily accessible by Joanne.

Those that go beyond have already helped themselves heal from past traumas, relive some lives or experiences, then gone on to other things — new lifetimes, for example. The way to view them, therefore, is as they were, in a kind of blueprint state that captures who they were when alive without needing update, in a sense. They are informed by the next level of consciousness. Therefore, the best information relating to each person is available with my help and others'.

I discovered how to do this while physical, and as a result wrote the afterlife journals of Rembrandt van Rijn, Paul Cézanne, and William James.[2] So while this has been done before, as you will see, it is just as special now as it was then.

Enjoy the book!

Jane Roberts

---

[2] *The World View of Rembrandt, The World View of Paul Cézanne: A Psychic Interpretation,* and *The Afterdeath Journal of an American Philosopher: The World View of William James* by Jane Roberts.

CHAPTER 1

Anthony Bourdain:
You Will Be Fine Wherever You Go

Anthony Bourdain (1956-2018) was an American chef, author, and host of travel programs that took us to wonderful places all over the world. His explorations of food – and the profound influence that sharing food has on humanity – made him an ambassador of cultural understanding. His suicide was a shock to many. He'd seemed so happy and "together." Why did he do it? I came across an interview[3] in which he said,

> I <u>want</u> to be happy. It's a perilous, selfish, foolish enterprise, believing in such things. But I think those platonic ideals are worth pursuing, in spite of everything that I've learned and done and seen. Life makes cynics of us all, especially when you travel as much as I do.

Coincidentally, I'd been exploring the idea that cynicism is frustrated idealism, something said of Machiavelli, who I'd been researching for a musical that Paul and I were writing. The day after Anthony died, I wanted to speak with him, but felt cynical and reluctant going into the session. I doubted my abilities. I doubted the value of doing it, and if I did, of sharing it. I thought "Few people will appreciate it, or believe me, some already think I'm nuts, why should I bother? How can I, or anyone, get past this, especially since it may have killed you?" He came through.

---

[3] Patrick Radden Keefe, "Travels with Anthony Bourdain," *The New Yorker*, June 8, 2018.

The way to see this is as an awesome ability to connect with others, which is what I did, too.

The way I'd suggest going forward is to consider what you do as fun. If you can't make it fun, try to find a way to see it as important. The way I had of getting around the globe had to do with fun first. Then it became less important as the years went by. It became harder to break the cycle of decent work to kill off my demons. It became more guided by trying to <u>avoid</u> something rather than trying to <u>go towards</u> something.

If you get rest, food, love, etc., you will find out where to go and what to do. I lost something beautiful along the way, which was good people around me more often. I was lonely on the road, as well as deeply depressed. I couldn't go into a restaurant without getting a lot of people focused on me. I didn't like that, so I kept running away from that.

I was not able to fully get to where I needed to be with regard to companions. I was not really wanting to commit to anything more than my daughter. So if I was escaping from something, it was me being down.

I can't express how very lucky I've been to have had the life I've led. There's nothing greater than doing things for people that you love. I expect people may be feeling down about my suicide because they are afraid, that they may need some more help avoiding depression, and that's a good thing. <u>If I helped people call somebody and not take their own life, it would be worthwhile</u>.[4]

---

[4] Suicide prevention call centers (1-800-273-8255 in the U.S.) are available in many countries, some specific to groups such as veterans and LGBT youth. They are staffed by trained, sympathetic

However, I don't really feel badly about it. I didn't call because I wasn't wanting to be talked out of it. I'd committed.[5]

Now in hindsight, I was not really having enough fun when I was physical. I was more into "doing things that are important," which will get you if you're not careful. <u>The fun has to be first</u>. So if you can take some of the bullshit of life because you're having fun, do it, because there's nothing better than that. If you look at yourself and your work as only important, this will get you in the end.

If I had to do it over again, I would have found a way to have more fun on the road, because that would have saved me. But I was battling a lot of mind tricks I played with myself. Looking for answers to big questions was a biggie. Don't become too invested in figuring things out. I did too much of that.

The expectations, too, were hard on me. I wasn't going to be privy to the life I needed because there were people relying on me that had to be paid. So this was a classic "I was living for others" scenario, which

---

people who can help. As you read this book, you'll hopefully realize that <u>suicide will not provide a permanent solution</u> to the pain we feel, for we bring our challenges with us into the afterlife. Please get the help you need <u>now</u>.

[5] Some months after this session, I asked Anthony about his experience directly after his suicide. "Afterwards, I was totally put off by what my body looked like when dead. I hadn't considered before that I would actually see myself. I was unprepared, too, for what would follow: a sort of movement—though I wasn't physical, so I wasn't <u>really</u> moving—into a kind of rehab place. Then I moved into the place I'm in now—the place of knowing more than I did when I was physical."

was not what I needed. I needed to be less lonely and having more fun. So do that.

If you want to say anything to people say this: I was not going to go further with my work. I was not going to have much more fun, either, because of my demons. However, I should have taken a cue from the life skills that I earned on the way: <u>look forward to the next day</u>.

That's what I should have done better. If I'd done that, I would have seen my way through a tough night. Do that. If you want to consider having fun, do that too. But don't feel badly about how the world is. There's a lot to be said about bad things happening, which has to do with growth and love for one another that's beyond our understanding.

The atmosphere of life here, where I'm at now, has to do with mercy for yourself and others, by default, because it all comes from you. If you need somebody to help you, there are people here. However, it's not to say anybody should check out. My work had grown in maturation to the point that I was able to say, "That's all I've got." That's what I meant earlier when I said my work had nowhere to go.

Forget about everything in the world that's wrong with it and just love it for what it is. This will help you move into a better place as somebody who is an idealist, because otherwise you will become cynical, which is a curse that I had, too.

This has to do with the importance thing, making the ills of the world bigger than they really are. For chrissakes, I got upset when I got bad hamburgers! This is what I'm talking about. Don't let that shit get you down.

Okay? How's that for a good read?

Thank you! I send you lots of love, as many do.

I feel that. I do. I don't have anything else to say except that I love the world that I had so many good times in. I look forward to having more fun times here, too. There's no end to what fun you can have in life, wherever that takes you. Take it from me, I'm here now without a paddle and I'm fine with it.

You will be fine wherever you go. Realize that and you will have the broad perspective that drew you to my work in the first place. Go forth and have fun with whatever it is you're passionate about. That served me well and it will serve you, too.

Can you advise me on how open I should be about this information? Should I share it?

I don't see the trouble you have with this, because this is who you are and it's fantastic. I even think I would be open another time to doing this again, because you have a lot of things to share.

For now, put it out there, but don't be attached to what it does with regard to its value to people. They are really lame sometimes! It's not you, darlin', it's more about them. So just let that shit go and do what you want to. Remember to have fun!

Okay, thank you.

It's been a pleasure. Have fun today.

Anthony Bourdain

CHAPTER 2

Hunter S. Thompson:
The Framework is Holy

I was very encouraged by Anthony Bourdain's session. It felt and sounded like him, and he said things that were helpful to me and the people I shared it with on my blog. I didn't pursue more sessions with dead people for some months. Then one morning around 4 a.m., in the most random way possible, something sprang from my subconscious, and I wanted to talk to Hunter S. Thompson. I'd read some of his work and admired him as a writer and thinker.

It was April 2020, and Donald Trump—who'd ridden a wave of hateful, divisive populism to "Make America Great Again"—was President of the United States. His administration—and the political interests that made it possible—encouraged white supremacy, misogyny, greed, and violence. The COVID-19 coronavirus global pandemic had created mass shutdowns the month before, and many of us were sheltering in our homes.

Hunter S. Thompson (1937-2005) was an American journalist, author, founder of "gonzo journalism" and prolific drug-imbiber who unflinchingly exposed the ugliness he saw in our culture. After a series of health issues, Hunter committed suicide by gunshot in his home. Johnny Depp allegedly spent $3 million on his funeral, which included firing his ashes from a cannon that had been hoisted atop a 47-meter tower on Thompson's Colorado farm. "He loved explosions," said Thompson's widow, Anita.

It turned out that my intuition to talk with Hunter wasn't unfounded, as he came right through. I would find out later that Anthony Bourdain was a huge fan of Hunter. Had he put us in touch?

I'm Hunter S. Thompson, middle name Surly. I was an informative travel host who pervaded the ink lines of media through journalism and books. My main claim to fame was a movie that claimed that I was a genius. However, I deny that accusation.

I want to share what I know with somebody who will hear what I have to say now that I'm in the bardo kind of place that you may think of as heaven. However, this is more of an ontologically fraught word. Heaven is where you find it, living or dead like me.

I'm forgetting a lot these days. Forgetting what life was like while physical because I haven't been down to earth for a while. Even while physical, my addictions kept me from behaving in any sense of the word "grounded." I did have fears about not being accurate or truthful enough. That's what kept me addicted.

What a world you live in now! When I was the person that I was, Hunter S. Thompson — which I have sort of shrugged off to become better and wider than when I was Hunter... having said that, I'm still Hunter... however, more of me is here now than when I was Hunter <u>only</u>, let's say — I was tripping my balls off frequently so as to get to where I have found myself now.

I wouldn't suggest this for just anybody. I wasn't the most spectacular person when doing this shit.

However, it did allow me a glimpse into the sorts of reality that <u>frames</u> your world but is not <u>in it</u>, necessarily.

The framework is holy. That's what I've found so far. The spectacular drugs that are now coming to the consciousness of many individuals have unique benefits in that they are spectacularly grooming whole generations to come with the sorts of stimulation that's required for the brain to be fully alive.

The carpenters of these concoctions are working in their huts now to stimulate not just the economy — however great that is — but the entire planet in a sort of self-congratulatory spectator sport in which eyes will be opened, hearts will be tamed to become the sorts of gentle giants they are, and the population of countries will shift towards new worldviews. I'm certain that the effects will be thrilling.

The sense of urgency you have about change is the same I had then. I wasn't able to fully realize the change in my lifetime, having had physical illnesses that impaired my ability to be in my body comfortably, which is why I offed myself. More about this later. However, my inner illness was real, too. I had not really gotten to the point where I was able to forgive myself for things I wasn't able to really get past — the sorts of misery that plague everybody — nor was I whole in the sense of forgiveness for others, either. These ramified themselves in my physical body.

There wasn't a smidgen of doubt that I was driving myself crazy with obsessive thoughts. I just didn't have the means to address them in ways that were truly helpful. The drugs were not always the answer. They were a crater in my soul, eventually, because they wouldn't help but hinder my ability to persuade myself to be real with myself for good.

So that's not something I'm proud of, but I did learn, and I'm saying to you: <u>don't let the drugs do you in</u>. They have a lot of benefits. They have a lot of nurturing qualities, too, because they will expand consciousness when done right. But I didn't always do them right, and I was not a happy camper too often because of that.

The figures of light they talk about are real here. They come and go like breezes drifting by. They console me often when I'm lounging about. I do this now—a lot—forgiving myself. Mostly I can hear them like whispers in my hearing, not that I have ears now. I don't. I hear them inside myself. This is something you will learn when you check out. You have this all inside you now, too. You only need to make sure you hold it dearly and pay attention.

So I'm sitting around here like a goat that's lost its pack without really much to do except to talk to people like you. There are others here like me, writers who want to talk to you, too. However, they want to be asked first.

I like that you asked me to do this. I have a lot of action here without there really being any action. But when it really comes down to it, I like that I can still talk to people this way without having to hear from anybody else that they don't like it. This will be a perfect setup: if they don't like it, you blame me and I'll blame you.

The facts are these. There really is an afterlife. I'm here. I don't know how long I have been here nor will be. The supervisors here are invisible. They wreck my soul with beautiful thoughts about me. However, I'm still myself, too, lounging about, smoking, getting high, only without the miracle drugs of the sixties and seventies.

I want you to hear me when I tell you this: <u>there's nothing else but you now</u>. There's nothing else but you now to pick up the slack of entire generations who have failed you. Have the courage and honesty to say what you think regardless of how people will take it. This was my credo when I was alive. It still works most of the time.

Sometimes you really do need to be kind to people, too. That wasn't my bailiwick either, although I did love deeply. Do that too.

Now in regard to your current administration: <u>throw the motherfuckers out</u>.[6] Throw them out. Take them down. Do whatever you can to subvert the system in whole ways. Think it through carefully.

Then do what you can to build a new world without all the bullshit. Don't build bunkers, build communities of people who help each other. Keep your farming and food sources local and keep your health care people local. Keep the businesses small if you can. There's nothing wrong with the businesses now, they just require oversight that you can't give right now because you have terrible leaders in office. Run for office. Make America <u>Really</u> Great again because you and I know it can be. Don't build arsenals like I did. Keep the faith in people. That's something I didn't do enough of.

---

[6] Trump was voted out of office the following November, and on the following January 6 incited a violent attack on the U.S. Capitol.

Then when the time comes, die peacefully knowing you did what you could.

Do what you can to heal yourself and others. This is something I could have done to save my life if I had been privy to the kinds of resources you have available to you now. I had no real spiritual guidance from outside. Yes, I had drugs. They were awesome teachers. You have others who speak from where I am now without needing to proselytize. Try getting yourself some spiritual help if you can.

I can't suspect there's anything wrong with doing this kind of channeling thing. This is heavy shit, man! The act of celebrating somebody by pulling them in to speak with you directly? How can that be possible? I can't think of any better way to connect with what you have to gain than to teach others what they are capable of in this manner.

The only thing left to say is that I have a deep love for the planet. I have always had this for as long as I can remember.

I have not done much more than to provoke people. Sometimes that's all you need to do. Just realize that provocation is the first step. You need sane people to hold steady as you look at the options you have. The only reason to feel unsafe is because you don't know who all these are yet. You will in time.

I have the sense there's going to be a lot of people doing what they can. You will be one of them if you want to. Then do whatever it takes to find out where to put your love and sanity, because there's going to be a lot of both required.

Party on.

Thank you, Hunter. Your family seemed to accept your suicide, and you'd spoken about it in the past. What was your mindset at the time, and would you consider it healthy? Were you aware of the funeral Johnny Depp gave you?

I want to share a few secrets about me. First off, I don't like spectacle. This would seem at odds with the spectacles I invented to further my writing in the sense of going gonzo, which for me was an unnecessary term if you really do believe that journalism is based on regular people having a spectacle-filled experience. This typically doesn't happen when you just sit around waiting for it. You have to create it. So I was invested in persuading people to go there for one thing and end up experiencing something totally different.

The spectacle was, therefore, not the same as the story. The Democratic National Convention of 1968 was indeed a spectacle that I reported on. However, there was no need to feel any differently when the spectacle that played out on the streets was the main story. I wasn't there to be part of a spectacle, just to report it.

The spectacles I invented were more about how to be wholly alive when boring things were going on. This was an offering to the gods of journalism. Everything I did was an offering to the gods of journalism. In my skepticism was the true story: that the things we look at are only a very small part of what's really going on underneath.

The spectacular story that was my life — now that I look on it from where I stand now — is only a sliver of the greater story that you're all living now.

Suffice to say, the funeral spectacle that Johnny put on for me was in every way beautiful. I couldn't have asked for a better sendoff. The beauty wasn't just in having my smattering of body parts shoved into the transparent night sky, only to be blasted into tiny, microscopic units of plasma and bone to fertilize the planet. I had to have some kind of presence in order to see it. Therefore, I was not only there in the people I loved, I was there in the fuselage barreling upwards, and I was there in the little bits of me that survived the explosion.

I was there, I'm here now, I will be around forever as far as I can tell. There's no unit of measurement for what I am now. I'm "chosen" in the sense of having had some kind of "credentials" to get to where I am now. However, I'm not sure I am anything different than I was before.

The reason I decided to kill myself — and yes, I did indeed do this myself — is that I wasn't having a very good time of it physically. Mentally, there wasn't a whole lot for me to feel sorry about. I was good mentally, I wasn't sure I wanted to keep living, that's all. I was shorn of my youth like some old crabby goat without any mountaintops to climb anymore.

Nothing interested me much except for life after death. This really did not interest me as much as it baffled me. There was a curiosity there that had to do with my immense desire to chronicle what that was like without needing to be physical again or to feel anything differently, but to be who I was, able to take some of myself with me without needing a body, or at least having a better one right away.

This is having some effects that were not considered before. I thought I might become nonphysical, but I didn't know I would still be physical in the sense of my body really is my body, just healing differently than when I was really physical.

The reason I saw this as "another kind of life only with a better body" is that this was my wish. I wasn't really aware of it yet. Now I know the place where I'm at now has properties that heal without this being automatic.

Do you follow? I've had to look at myself deeply, which I didn't do as well while alive.

Now I'm happy just to get up in the morning because the mornings are wonderful. There is a time sense — "timeless cycles" is probably the better term — without long weeks that stretch into nowhere. It's as if the ground has shaken itself out and cascaded itself across my path in ways that are eternal without losing any of its beauty. The forests are forests, the trees look like they are supposed to look, and everything is immaculately certain about itself, not probable, but whole, vibrant, effusive.

The indications of something better beyond here are non-existent. There's not any of the religious crap here, just cold hard truth that's ephemeral as well as timeless. It's like walking into a bar and ordering one of everything, and having a bottomless stomach for everything, too.

That's what awaited me when I died. I wasn't quite ready to drink, or inhale, this. I needed to open myself up to it while learning how to do that. The act of breathing wasn't breathing as much as allowance for everything, so that when I was able, I could step into a kind of surface-level world where everything goes on forever — every bud of the tree — without the regular thoughts of anything dying ever again.

That's what I have going on now. When you die, you will have similar experiences. You will not have the same as me, you will have your own. You'll create whatever world you want to create. It's easy to do and you don't need to pay for it ever again. How great is that?

The only other thing I want to mention is when I died, I left some people with questions about why I did it. The way I want them to see this is as an effort on my part that was worth it. This wasn't something I'd ever take lightly, and they know that. They know that I wasn't going to be careless about this.

However, I would have not done so in a way that left my body there. I would have done it differently without them having to find me. That's the only thing I regretted afterwards and want to just say I'm sorry about that. I loved you all. Immediately following the trigger pull, I was able to see what I had done without knowing for sure where I was. When I looked back on the scene, I was regretful you had to see it, too.

The funeral, therefore, was a brilliant spectacle to end my life, really. That's how I want to be remembered, and I think it was a fine gesture by someone I was fully able to call my brother.

Rest in peace, you all, whether or not you are dead yet, and I will see you at the big rodeo in the sky.

A week or so later, I sat down to do another transmission, letting the Committee suggest who would come through next. It was Hunter, and I wasn't surprised since, after all, he'd said he had an "immense desire to chronicle" what life after death was like.

I have a lot of things to say about what's happening in the world now, so may I proceed?

Yes, of course.

I have not come so far in the world only to <u>not</u> say what I have learned now that I'm dead. "The imparting of wisdom" may not be the best words to describe this memento — you might say — of my life, this inner sense of what's needed in the world now, besides what you know already, truth, love, etc. These things only get you so far.

The way I like to think about what I've done on Planet Earth is as frightening at times, and lovely, too. These things aren't that different, really. The news I have to impart is going to be excellent, so stay tuned, because I'm still recovering as a war correspondent of the world and will have more to say from my bed here in the Galaxy Hotel.

The reason for my efforts to withdraw from your world has had similar consequences now that I'm undead. The undeath is not the same as death. You might consider me, even, still alive without a body.

What the world has done to people is what the world did to me. I was breaking up inside all the time without any reason to believe that where I was going was real in the sense of fantasy vs. reality. The path for me was unreal, in so many ways, that I had to consider that maybe this war of the worlds that is going on now would never end: the war being, of course, between the literal and figurative, the Nazis and the Parliament, the fornicators and the nuns, the effortless and the effortful, those extreme cases of envy and those great acts of giving. The point being: <u>these are extremes only</u>.

The reason I have for saying these things is what I want to share now that I know this: <u>these are illusory</u>.

The things in life that seem like extremes really aren't. They are gifts with different wrappings, all necessary to giving you the experiences on the planet that you came here for.

I can't recall any day in which I sheltered in place without feeling a bit like I was taking shelter from the war, you might say. I was healthy, physically, until I had too many reasons to want to stay put.

The path for me, therefore, wasn't the path for others who only want to run around and play in the sunshine. I wasn't that kind of person, really. I liked, and still like, to be home with my guns and my wishes for a better tomorrow.

What I was not seeing then that I'm seeing now is the polar opposites playing with your minds in ways that you don't have to buy into. The detergent is the same as the dirt. The efforts of the evil are the same as the efforts of the good. The spanking new projects are wrapped in the skins of the debris on which they are built.

So when you just say to yourself "that's good" or "bad," you excuse yourselves from the worst things, you think, because you don't have the capacity to explore why you think this. The capacity is there, you don't use it. You say, "this is not <u>this</u>" and "this is not <u>that</u>." However, <u>this is all that</u>, <u>this is all that</u>, <u>this is all that</u>.

See what I mean? You have to get past the judging about everything that you have in front of you. See things as filled with light, regardless of what color the light is.

This is not something easy to do right away, however. You need to invoke the kinds of religious feeling that you portray as wrong or bad at times. See what I mean? You sometimes deny yourselves even the opportunity to be whole with the world. You need to stop judging so much.

That's what I have decided to share with you as my memento of the war on earth which, as you can see, isn't really that. The war is in your mind only, not even in the world.

See how that works, this wonderful way of viewing things as filled with light? See how that goes? Because you can't really tell anybody what's what until you see yourselves as whole, and to do that requires your perspective to widen, some days more than others. You'll want to really pay attention to what's in front of you.

See how very willing you have been to dismiss or realize some kind of effort to withstand the forces of what you consider wrong for some goddamned reason that is mostly wrong in itself?

So don't do what I did. See things as beautiful regardless of what color of light they are and be damned to do anything differently because ultimately you will be damned if you do. You will be in the hell of your own making.

Now, that said, there are some reasons to, coincidentally, remain calm in the face of terror. You <u>do</u> have certain elements to play with when physical, like those who want to kill you, for example.

The way I would approach these elements — and I do mean elements, these are not necessarily people, they can be forest fires — is to tell them to <u>please back off</u>. That's all. Just please back off. Be polite, then if they don't do what you want them to do, tell them they will need to stop that or will be fined a hundred dollars. That'll teach 'em!

Because ultimately there's nothing wrong with a forest fire, there's nothing wrong, really, with somebody holding a gun to your head, because you can't really know what the purpose of that is when you're in that situation.

So just lighten up, people! There will be terrible things that happen on the planet. The point of this will be to eventually have things better for more people.

Now, when you encounter somebody doing damage to yourself and property, I will suggest doing what's legal only without, hopefully, harming anybody. This means something, too, in the Great Plan. This is important — to not harm others and to help them if you are able — without going too far into the land of martyrdom that you sometimes think you have to in order to be whole. You don't.

So I'm not saying don't do things that are considerate, or even courageous, I'm just saying to not stifle your own instincts right out of the gate because something terrible is happening. Be there for it because this, too, will be something for you to enjoy in ways that you don't see yet.

The facts remain that the life you're living has reasons to be lived and has as much beauty in it than anything you might expect based on what you see as beautiful. The reasons for bad things happening is to enjoy them, too, while you are physical.

This sounds odd, for sure. Why would you want bad things to occur when there are so many beautiful rainbows and sunsets? Because that's what you chose when you decided to be wholly, physically attuned towards the earth. That comes with the territory, literally. So enjoying some bad days is not really an odd thing when you consider they will be all you might have on certain days. See?

The expectation that everything's going to be peaches is the problem. Without this expectation, you would be having a lot more fun every day. Instead, you get all bound up in the face of anything bad, in your view, that crosses your path.

What I'm saying is to light your path with your own beautiful light, to see everything as whole, and let yourselves enjoy whatever comes your way, because ultimately that's what your world will give you: <u>what you need</u>. And that, my friends, will not be what you want all the time.

Let me say just one more thing about the light of the world. You may think that you're so very connected when you do things like meditate, or listen to wonderful people on your audio tapes, or whatever you do to feel like your consciousness is so much higher than others. This is bullshit. This does not have anything to do, really, with life sometimes.

The facts are that being whole does not require you to be anything except who you have been all along, even with all the dumb stuff you have done, and the dumb stuff maybe you're still doing.

The ascended masters are not the only ones who have something to give you. Each person in your path, each tree, has something to give you when you allow it to. All you have to do is appreciate that they are there for you.

Then breathe in each day with complete acceptance without thinking that you will be anything but somebody who is wonderful — whatever you do — and let the forces guide you towards your own fun and challenging day.

Go forth and be whole, you all.

With love from Hunter

CHAPTER 3

Ayn Rand:
Atlas Continues to Carry the World

Hunter's transmission seemed like the continuation of his work as a journalist, only this time covering the afterlife. His description of my process of engaging authors shocked me: "There are others here like me, writers who want to talk to you, too. However, they want to be asked first." I was skeptical at first but knew that I did have something to do with who came through. I decided to try to speak with Ayn Rand, who I'd never read but had spoken to briefly in 2013 after I saw a movie about her and felt empathically connected.

Ayn Rand (1905-1982) was a Russian-American writer known for her best-selling novels — The Fountainhead *and* Atlas Shrugged *— and for developing a philosophical system she called Objectivism. Rand was a pure materialist who advocated reason as the only means of acquiring valid knowledge, certainly not the psychic means used to create this book! Her work is often criticized as encouraging selfishness and greed and cited as an influence of the U.S. political right.*

There seemed to be a protocol being followed by the previous authors to provide a chapter each, but Ayn wanted to do an entire book, immediately. This created a challenging situation not unlike negotiating on a used car. Still, I'm glad she pushed, for what follows is an extraordinary transmission. Ayn was an atheist who didn't believe in the afterlife, then found herself in it, and tells us about it. She also provides her views to help set the record straight about her work. It was important to me that she be allowed to do that, hence the lengthy chapter. Her books were lengthy, too, perhaps due to her Benzedrine (amphetamine or "speed") habit, which she also talks about here.

There was a bit more to life than I'd thought, because as you know, I was not in any way interested in what came after death, or what came between the breaths I took, or what came before life began. Of course, I was not easily influenced by anything that supposed that life was something beyond this physical life as you know it. But I do believe now that life begins long before birth – and always has been – and sense I have always known it has, although not in the personal sense of the word, perhaps.

I was not accepting of life's premise beyond what I knew in my physical life. Now that I'm not physically adept, let's say – because I am physical, in an odd sense of the word – I'm potentialized rather than potentialized with physicality. I'm not potentialized physically, but in mass, sensing all around me as One in ways I had not had the experience of before. This may sound odd coming from me, because I was so very bound with physicality – while I was alive on the planet, that is. I am not as bored with life now as I was sometimes on earth, in between things I was doing. Sometimes I became bored with life, sometimes I was depressed.

Now I am not at all bored or depressed. I'm singing around the place I call my "protocol place," meaning I have a protocol that keeps me sane in the sense of constructing my realities with vigor rather than with some degree of chaos that I find irritating in this place.

My protocol place has in some ways helped me to let go of my fears that I was not as great an author as I would have liked to have been. I don't need to be that anymore. I can realize more patience with myself, now that I'm not the way as I was before, with my sense of urgency. I'm not urgent like that anymore. I have pains that I'm trying to get loose of, and I have my husband Frank here, too, to keep me company.

I don't have anything else to say except that I'm pleased to make the connection with you. I have a lot of things I'd still like to say about the world as it is, and I would rather do so with you than with other types of individuals who don't get the words down on paper.

(While she was "talking," our cat, Rumi, started yowling like crazy.) Thank you! What might I call you? Miss Rand?

Call me Ayn. I like the name and I like to hear it even if only in your mind, my dear.

The scope of the work I'd like to do would be great, because I have a lot of things I'd like to say. There may be things you won't like about what I have to say because I truly haven't changed my mind about some things.

I do believe the world would be a better one for all if my ideas were embraced in the ways I would have liked for them to. That said, the reasons they were not embraced had to do with the nullification of those individuals who would not be privy to the sorts of resources that the individuals who would benefit the least have. In other words, those in power were not the ones I sacrificed my life for to teach — about how each individual can have more of life than they had been taught was possible.

What aspects of the teachings of mine were truly wrong? None, as far as I can tell. The responsibility for unity is always going to be with each individual. That was something that was not as sharpened in my mind as it should have been. Therefore, the results of my work have been tragically endorsed by those in power as a way to keep people in chains of economic deficiency, lack of full resources, and inequitable practices that I feel terrible about now.

The teachings were not fully brought to the world in "whole" ways. Yes, I do consider them teachings more than anything. The practical words have influenced many individuals as to what to do every day of their lives. If that's not teaching, what is?

This was my fault entirely. I take responsibility for the convergence of the right wing of the governmental influences taking charge in ways that were not at all performed with unity. The unity was embraced instead by those who had rejected what I had to say about the selfishness required to live a full life. The purpose, therefore, of my writing now has to do with the innocent people who are suffering due to the lack of understanding of what I said. I'd like to create a new book to set them straight.

Wow, I'm honored that you want to write a book with me, but I can't commit to it right now. Can we do a lengthier chapter that includes the most important information?

I understand that to commit to writing a book the size of *Atlas Shrugged* would not be realistic for you now, or ever, for that matter. I wouldn't ask you to do that. The point is to set the record straight, to help people who would benefit from reading this work. We can call it something like *Atlas Continues to Carry the World: An Afterlife Reading from Ayn Rand.*

The point of this is to set the record straight about what I have accomplished while physical, what I have learned since not being physical, and what I have in store for my life now that I have gone beyond your physical world into new types of expression.

This has been a wonderful way to get past the shortcomings of not having an earth body: to talk through somebody who is so open to me that I can move her fingers on her typewriter keys. The world has changed to such a degree since I died that it moves me even to see her sitting there with another kind of computer that stretches in every direction — woman-powered, throughout the time-space continuum, throughout the internet that you call it — into the vast realms both heavenly as well as earthly.

The planet has remarkable technological capability now that the world has realized more unity. This unity is what I will discuss in my book that she is now writing with me. She's my fingers, my arms, but I have control over her thinking in ways that are amazingly similar to how I was able to channel my own thoughts when I was a writer.

I do not think I had anything better than she, really — an old typewriter, some Benzedrine much of the time, that was stimulating my mind in ways that were not always beneficial to what I was typing. However, this was calming for me in an abstract way.

The speed — this diabolical kind of switch that gets turned on when one is in the throes of too much laziness of mind — held me fast in its embrace while I was able to succeed at getting my thoughts out on paper. The speed was ultimately not the best conversationalist, though this was factoring in my gains of thought that I wanted to express, the gains of thought being what I had to share.

The speed detracted from the thoughts because the speed broke down things in ways that were openly hostile at times. Speaking quickly, pounding typewriter, I had to succumb to the darker forces of my world — hating how I felt, loathing the world at times to the point of distraction. The world was not clueless, as I had hoped. I would set forth something that would straighten everybody out without thinking that I could not actually do that.

Therefore, the forces of Benzedrine complied with my inner devotion to chaos as well as order. "Take more speed to get the words out, take more speed to get the words out..." became my cause without knowing that the words were being stoked in the fear zones of my mind to "better" people. The "betterment of people" was my credo. I did not realize at the time that the betterment of people had a lot of potential pitfalls which I wish to address now.

I can't determine now what made me so deterministic in my reasoning that life had to correspond to what I was thinking it should. I can't determine either if I was a junkie who wanted only to tell others what to do, rather than addressing my own haphazard world, or if I was truly inspired to let go of whatever I had addressed in order to be a better mum to the world.

The motherly aspects of my life were affected by my own decisions to be fully carefree — loose with my morality at times—and to codify in words of generosity my own shortcomings of faithfulness, for example. The reason I mention these attributes of myself is, I can't think morally now while claiming to know more than I know. I can say with certainty I was not always right about this.

I was regarded as an optimist by some individuals, a pessimist by other individuals, as a hostile person by some, and as a loving person by others. This has to do with the religious beliefs of those who were doing the assuming about what I was bringing into the world.

The facts are that I was <u>not</u> religious in the way that others were. I <u>was</u> religious in other ways, though, in ways that were characteristic of somebody who really wanted to do right in the world. The shepherd holding his flock was, for me, a cruel image made by religious authorities to keep people bridled, controlled, and dominated by religious clerics.

I was not going to stand for that as long as I lived. I would work to counter that sort of groupthink. The path for me was to take down this kind of cruel encumbrance on the population. This was drawn from governmental aspects that I witnessed in Russia. That path was not the path I would take.

Fortunately, I would move to the next country that had me in its thrall—The United States of America. Given the opportunity to live there, I was fascinated by the charter of the country to provide that which I had been denied in Russia: the ability to pursue one's happiness. This was regardless of what the religions said. This was regardless, too, of what even the father of the house said.

This was pure fun for a girl who would travel the world with her ability to shell out her own thoughts on the subject. This took me to places I had never even imagined in my world. I was the best person I could be, the best person I could imagine to take this on.

In this way, I <u>was</u> a religious person: a person who was in every way somebody who had devotion to my cause to liberate individuals from the sinking ship of religious interests who had their worst ambitions at play.

This was the best person I could be. If I faltered in my challenge, I would at least have tried harder than perhaps anybody to insinuate my thoughts into the world so others may see the relativistic nature of communal living with regard to control, chaos, and dominance. This would be my life's work and I fulfilled it brilliantly.

What I did not realize was how — with every step of my life — I had to come to terms with the affects that grew from my work, how planted in the soil these ideas became, and what was yielded from them. I'm wishing to address those now.

The forfeiting of my will to engage the world has been the most difficult thing for me during this transition of physical to nonphysical in the sense of patriarchy still ruling the world. I have this still sticking in my heart like a thorn.

To take up where I left off while physical is the best path, I think, with regard to this work now. (I ultimately will want to capture a few more ideas as we go; however, the greatest gift I can give is to allow this to be captured in the shortest form possible so as to get more readers. This has not always been my gift—

brevity, that is—so I will do what I can to make this shorter than usual.)

This has been the most fascinating thing, these articles of impeachment of your president.[7] He has not been the most articulate person, which has been tremendously frustrating for those like me who like things articulated in verbs, nouns, and adjectives.

His spurious comments—like what he tweets—are addictive for those who like the crass materialism of everyday life: the car commercials, the bank loan ads, the flattering hordes of those who follow movie stars and other pseudo-thinkers that hold sway in your world.

This is not the jargon of those who are educated, in other words. The educated people of your world do not deal in these things very often. They know when they hear the words of somebody like Donald Trump that there's a snake in the grass of freedom when that person holds high office, or even has resources that will take advantage of good people.

This is not the person I was talking to in my books! I thought I was talking to those who were educated. Therefore, my books reached people in ways they were not ready for: ruthless, cunning people who used them as indulgences for their own stupid, shortsighted ends. Because, ultimately, it is stupid to believe that selfishness will win the day. This is not what I wanted to impart to the world.

---

[7] Then-president Donald Trump had been impeached the previous December (2019) for abuse of power and obstruction of Congress. The Senate acquitted him in February 2020, three months before Ayn wrote this chapter. He would be impeached and acquitted again the next January and February (2021).

What I wanted to impart was that freedom relies on individuals who aggressively take charge of their lives to make themselves happy, foremost. This was not the most successful way to reach people, though.

Ultimately, the people who needed to read my books were those who were pummeled by religious beliefs that kept them reinforced in the ultimate lie: that they were no good, that they were not even the best individuals for their lives. How insulting that was to the ultimate God of whoever was needing to hear this most: the true God if there is one!

The work I was able to put into pages was, therefore, not accessible to those who needed to break free: people who were not highly educated nor drawn to reading eight hundred-page books.

This was malarkey to some individuals who had gone beyond, to thinking that they were impervious to religion if they chose to be. They were not in my readership either, because they did not need to rely on someone like me telling them they should have no worries, that there was no hell, and there was not even a heaven, and it was alright if they did not want to believe in the "sin vs. no sin" rationale for the afterlife experience.

This was cautioned in the religious world as the means to control people. I resisted this with every fiber of my being, knowing that in the hands of the government—which religion played a big part sometimes—there would be hell to pay when joined into battle for some cause that was unifying only in the sense of creating a stronger state. This was anathema to me.

The Trumps of the world know that they can take on the role of the religious cleric who tells everybody what to do. This has to do with God, too, because you still have the legacy of old, wise male idols who capture the attention of those needing strong paternal influences. The perfect storm is when the paternal figure is a devil like Trump. This exists in many forms on your world: you've created discarnate devils and incarnate ones, too.

And this is the point to consider, that even if you see yourselves as needing a firm patriarchal figure in your lives, you can have one any time by reinforcing your own sense of justice. This is the legacy of the male god—justice—not only in the sense of sending bad guys to hell and good ones to heaven but invoking a world of justice for all when the male god is truly divine in the sense of goodness personified. It's not outside of any of you. I had this sense when I was alive, too, because I was very masculine in my verbiage, my thinking, my sense of self as boss of myself. I was patriarchal, too, in my own way. I sought justice for what I found to be corrupt patriarchy.

So it was my choosing to embark on the path of taking on this old, worn-out god of Abraham, and invoking in my own works the god I thought everybody needed: the God of Love of Self. That was my point. However, that was what got corrupted, and I have regrets about that. I don't want to continue to talk about this because I have so many other things to share, so I will do that now.

This president, therefore, represents the worst in the model of patriarchy, without knowing it, of course. He's not aggressively unrealized—just stubbornly unrealized—capable of doing some very bad things in his term of office. This will be the result, therefore, of religion gone bad, too, because it has provided this model of God, this currency of rhetoric that assumes everyone has to hit the ground running in their lives, too, to be special, to be competent at taking advantage of others for one's own greed.

This is where I wish I would have said something differently than I did. For in getting to where people need to be, you <u>never</u> have to take advantage of somebody.

This was something I learned later in life while I was physical: that I was able to get what I needed without trampling on somebody else. This was something, too, that individuals who read my books didn't quite follow because they needed to find out how to get past their own sets of authority, sometimes needing to trample on those who kept them down.

This type of action is constantly being exploited by those who want to provoke individuals to rise up against government officials who mean well. They say that it's wrong for them to tell us what to do, when the reality is, they aren't taking on the ones who started this in the first place: the religious who take advantage of them, the landlords who take advantage of them, too. So, the point is, yes, take on those who are taking advantage of others and need to be stopped. However, that is misapplied to those who aren't really doing that.

The philosophy of Objectivism, therefore, has some shortcomings when one is exposed to the reality of the world. It assumes that in every case there is some win for people who follow completely rational thinking in getting their desires, when in reality, sometimes we can't have our desires. Sometimes we can't even get what we really need. Then what? Your life's path will show you what you need then help you get that.

Now, a few words about the afterdeath environment, or my favorite protocol place, as I call it. The protocol place where I am now is not the darkest place in hell, as many have chosen to send me in their thoughts. This is a joke because you know I <u>did</u> like to laugh sometimes!

I live somewhere now that has many floors to it. Some floors are huge, some are small. The protocols have to do with accessing these floors. The reason I mention this is, I'm aware that Hunter S. Thompson provided this idea [in Chapter 2]. The "access credentials" he mentions are like this idea of floors. I'm where he is now in some ways, not in other ways. This is drawing us together—this work you're doing. However, we're in different areas of consciousness. (He's wanting for me to mention now, too, he's looking to talk with you again so I will pass that along and will continue.[8])

The areas of consciousness I'm in now are floors that reach through other floors into spaces of light and darkness, as well as tone, color, and other attributes not quite realized in earthly terms. These areas are inspired by our mental state, our spiritual state, our healing state. Each floor has multiple corridors that go on forever. The actual places are not this linear, they are more ideas that move one about in new ways all the time.

Therefore, because of the chaos of this that I don't like very much, I have called this the "protocol place."

---

[8] I did speak again with Hunter, the transcript of which became the last section of Chapter 2.

It extends forever, too, so you can imagine why individuals want to take some measure to live with some form.

The protocol for me is like this: I have a space where I think and write. The writing isn't writing as much as it is committing words to lengthy passages of formless thoughts. The chapters are chapters, the books are books. I'm writing a book now that's being recorded by somebody who is physical. I don't have anybody else today that I do this with. However, there are potentials for that. My reality is, therefore, full of potentials: too many. It's like being physical, only so very erratic that you can't predict, for example, that when you take a step, your foot will move across a floor.

Therefore, I have maintained a protocol that says, "I can move across the floor anytime I want without needing to feel chaotic or out of control." This is something I decided to create to help me with my writing, and my life here with Frank, although he has some protocols that are different than mine. He observes more than I do outside his set of protocols: he sees things. I feel them more than see them, then I write. He's been an incredible help to me throughout my life and I would not want to be here without him. However, there's no reason to believe he's with me all the time, either. He has his protocols where he gets to play with others without causing harm to me. I have the same protocol.

Do you see? It's as if the protocols I set forth in my life were treasured so much that I created them here, too. In fact, I was intuiting these, I believe, when I was alive, creating the sort of lifestyle choices based in individual need rather than in religious or culturally acceptable ways. This has been a fun journey, each day getting to play with whoever I want without having to feel I'm doing anything to harm somebody else.

How joyful it is here! How expressive of my desires it is here! I have enough food, shelter, etc., to feel continually at peace—something you don't have the luxury of having, however I'm not sure this is a bad thing.

There's something about the delicacy of life, the challenge, the danger, that sets your world so right by my reasoning. It's like the path has many little barbs on it that you can see as effective in moving you to other paths or not. Each barb, each time you choose something better, you have enough things to move you to become happier as people that you really can't go wrong when you trust the world to show you your path. That's something I didn't really understand when physical.

There's not any reason to fear so much as long as you're able to enjoy where you're at and let the world move you to where you need to be. This has worked well for me here, although I would have done things similarly on earth if having this intellect had allowed me more realization of rest and relaxation. This has been my biggest joy now, here in this place of rest. I find many suitors for my attention and enjoy them all tremendously. You will find many ways to be deliciously enjoying your life, too, without having to worry too much about anything.

If there's any one thing I regret—besides not fully realizing the works being put into the hands of those who would not completely understand what I was saying because they were not well educated — it would be that I did not get enough rest. This is about the best thing you can do while physical. Be active, yes. However, rest is so very underrated that I feel I must share this so that individuals know that the restfulness you crave can be accomplished while physical. In doing so, you will find more promise in your days, as the struggle for you to stay awake while doing things you don't enjoy is breaking your spirits. Rest helps by indicating that you have reserves in you that you don't fully enjoy as much as you could.

In respect to my upbringing, I had the deepest, most profound experiences during my time in Russia. The days were full of the most expressive qualities of mankind: poetry, history, art. Reality was a blur of posthumous writings by the greatest of all thinkers including the Greeks Aristotle, Plato, and more. The reason I say this is, the writings were handed down from those who had passed on, so why is this collaboration [between physical and nonphysical people] any different than getting a copy of Aristotle's *Poetics* in the mail?

When asked to be contrite about having access to those greatest men at such a young age — because you know the proletariat had to be condemned for having thoughts of freedom the way some are in your country — I had not any reason to doubt that the minds of people had to be emancipated from this thinking.

To suggest that the works of these great men, mostly, were somehow wrong was of the deepest concern for me. Therefore, not only was I supplanted by the revolutionary forces, but you also have this going on now. You have areas of domestic terror now saying you can't behave according to what you've been taught, or no one has the education that we have, or there's nothing to learn besides what we have to teach you. A shameful poverty of thought has begun to take hold of your country now!

What I suggest mainly, then, is to coordinate with others to provide children the best educations that you possibly can. Read the classics. Learn from those who sought to overthrow fascism. In this, Waldorf education has the backbone to carry forth the messages of brotherhood, unity, and the basic idea that all people enjoy the world without regard to race or religion. This is heady stuff. Not enough of these schools exist. I knew about them, of course, when I was alive. Now I see the Waldorf education as paramount to everything that has to go forward to create the world you need to create.[9]

Without the forces of injustice having their hold on you, without the need for violence, you will find out exactly what the future holds by only doing one thing, and that is to realize your own potential.

This was something I had to learn the hard way when on your planet. The differences with the way of the world and the way of children growing up are these: you have to provide age-appropriate doses of

---

[9] Waldorf Education strives to develop artistic, intellectual, and practical skills in a holistic manner. The first Waldorf school opened in 1919 in Stuttgart, Germany, and while the Nazis closed Waldorf schools in Europe in the 1930s, there are now hundreds of them around the world. My husband, Paul, has been a Waldorf class teacher in Pacific Palisades, California, since 2012. So Ayn's mention of Waldorf made me wonder if she got this from me, but it is likely that she knew of Waldorf education while physical.

reality for children. Nothing comes closer to destroying the resources within them than coddling. The prototypes of how they will behave in their futures are created when they are children. <u>Stop coddling your children</u>!

The other idea that has to do with martial forces is this: coddled children are the ones who strike the greatest fear into the hearts of others, because they have not learned that their actions have consequences. This applies to Kim Jun Un as well as Donald Trump. These are children with dangerous toys who have been given everything they have wanted in life and will never be satisfied, for they will never learn how to be responsible for another person. So don't spoil or coddle your children because <u>there's too much at stake</u>!

The wonder of your world has been the most exciting thing for me to view from here, in the kind of space that you may think of as imagination. However, imagination is not the only force that guides my vision of what you have on today, for example. It's also reality in the inner sense of the word. You have a dark jacket on with a purple shirt, below there are dark trousers. Did you have to look to see if you were wearing dark trousers?

I didn't look, and that was fairly accurate. I'm wearing a black buttoned sweater over a purple top, and black sweatpants.

I didn't look either. Like you, I had only to use my inner senses. You attribute this knowing to your own remembrance of putting on your clothes.

Now what do you think I'm wearing today? You think it's something red.

Yes.

And you would be correct. The red dress sparkles with light, too. So I can see you, and you can see me, too, to some degree. What about me has you so competent in reaching me rather than others you might want to reach? It's my tone. My name has something to do with that.

The past few years have been showing you all what the world <u>should</u> be like without being quite like it now. What is it that you want from the world? What do you want the world to be like next year, or in twenty years? If you were to name something that was part of your world that is not part of your world now, what would it be?

The environment would be healthy, cared for, respected. That's truly the wish of all individuals without knowing it, even. The path of righteousness — and I mean that in the most morally sustainable way possible — is that the environment should be clean, cared for, respected, shared, without the need to do extractions of oil, coal, or anything that disrupts its natural cycles. The beauty of the world is something all can enjoy: that's why the people who are harming it really don't want to do that, deep down. What keeps them shackled is the fear they will not have enough of something. This is irrational as well as devastating to all concerned.

The wish of many is to restore the planet. However, the fears are that the world will not provide what you need unless you take it from her. This is the most blatant kind of sexism there is, for Mother Nature has feminine Divinity in her, as well as the procreative capacities that are beyond your comprehension. The planet has the most sophisticated means of turning dead into living, water into wine, so to speak.

What about the potential for the earth to recover is now taking your habits by storm? The pandemic. I'll say a bit about this.

The coronavirus pandemic[10] is supported by the notion that the earth needs to restore itself to what it needs to be to support life. The planet is not punishing you: the planet is providing you the best kind of change possible. Unless you go through this change, you will not have a planet left to live on. Without this change, you will not learn to appreciate the fullness that is your earth.

The beauty of the world can be viewed from your bedroom window. You don't need to go anywhere to feed yourself if you are so choosing. You don't have to be significantly wealthy to enjoy your life. You only need the basics: food, water, air, friends, and the education that is beginning to show itself, too. For in your need to satiate yourself without the usual junk food of bad programs and novelty performances, you

---

[10] The pandemic was in full force when this was written in May 2020. With so many people housebound, one benefit was that the environment was showing improvement, with large decreases in air and water pollution. Also, being housebound, people were able to pay greater attention to the essentials: their homes, families, foods, and how they spent their time. Many of us watched more film and TV programs, some "nourishing" and some "junk food."

will begin to go to the masters of education for the food for your brain. Some are doing this now without feeling hungry for anything else. This is satisfying you.

So, in your efforts to build a new world, allow yourselves to <u>consider building better educational systems for all — not only your children</u> — so you can learn to be whole again in body, mind, and spirit, too.

The reasons for us committing to writing this, therefore, are to show you how you can turn off the kinds of pursuits that I had pushed into the public consciousness — things that coalesced around a Superman kind of ego that could do anything he set out to do — so as to enjoy better pursuits.

This Superman is an old model, one worth pushing back into the forties and fifties, to get a sense of the appropriate context of my books, which were for <u>those</u> times, not <u>these</u> times. Those old books will continue to be sold, of course, but would be better understood in the context of their times, and not as manifestos for doing things that hurt others, as we said, as some have used them for this purpose.

The path, therefore, to help you out of this bind of selfish vs. unifying beliefs is to simply rely on yourself for what you can, reach out to others for what you need, then draw a big circle around the community you have created by simply being who you are. The way to invite the kinds of people you need into your lives is to be whole as best as you can. If you can't be whole, find others who will support you in your journey towards wholeness.

Then look at yourself with beautiful hearts, the kind of hearts that love each other's faults, too, and let yourself feel this love. For in your brains, hearts are not qualified to make these kinds of changes, but in your heart, you know they are. The brain will only choose what you think is the best choice, and this does not work in the way you think it does. See how that works? The brain needs the heart to move it along day by day, minute by beautiful minute, provoking the acts and works of generosity that you came here to cocreate — yes, cocreate.

This is what you are missing: <u>cocreation</u>.

Each day that passes in your time, I experience as well — in spiritual time, you might call it. The days flow around the clock like yours do, just differently. Some days will be different than others.

The cycles, therefore, are very much a part of this reality creation, ensuring a sort of change while being constant — while being, also, very expanding towards what each of us will want to pursue that day. I have days where I can see the ocean, I have days in which I can see the trees of Norway, I have days in which I can see everything in the world at what might be called a "peak of the Universe" experience.

There are no words to adequately describe what this feels like. If I had to choose, I would say the stratosphere is mine now. With every bit of my heart and soul, I cherish every day here as I did the earth, too. Only now I have the wisdom as well as consistency of temper to allow myself more fondness for everything, ever.

You tend to do the same thing. You see yourselves as embittered, striving, heartless at times, when the reality is, you're just normal people. Each time you feel sad, you say to yourself "I must get past this feeling" when the reality is that you just need to rest a bit, tell yourselves how wonderful you have been in the past, that you will be so in the future, and let the comforts of the world do that: <u>comfort you</u>.

The challenge of my life was very much about this kind of madness, a kind of solidarity with those who would be successful. The success, of course, was frequently about possession of one thing or another. Now I won't have any more of these kinds of thoughts of needing things I don't need. Now I can truly realize what life is about: <u>enjoyment</u>.

The creation, therefore, is never that. The creation of what you might think of as a life is never just that. The creation is always going to be cocreation. The purpose of life is to realize that there are multiple forces going through all things without rest, without even needing to slow down. The forces are indefatigable, with not any reason to slow, ever.

These forces create my world here, too, without my needing anything besides the persistence of reality I have here now. I love these forces more than I did when I was physical. The forces are matured to the point where they imbibe a respectful sense of purpose. With each flow of life, with each breath that you take, you pull these forces into your body to allow your next breath.

This is not something to take lightly. This is something worth dying for: the dying to life as you think it has been, then <u>resurrecting yourself as a new person each day you're alive</u>.

In this, each day will be a new day with your dying to self every evening, waking without fear, and going about your life without needing to hold anything in or down about yourself. The pressure of getting in the way of the forces it prohibits is what causes illness, of course. The flows are there, you need to see them with your heart to know what they are doing for you.

Each creative act allows freedom of flow, so you can think of the flows as mediating in spite of what you may think about this. The flows know you, know your situation in every second. The flows primarily attune to your body and spirit, and the mind is the last to know what's going on. Do you follow? Your <u>body</u> and <u>spirit</u> are more attuned to the artistic flows than your <u>mind</u>.

How's that for a complete reversal of my thinking when I was physical? In my stories, I had near to nothing to say about spiritual things, except for those forces that created the mind as well as its processes. There was no distinction, really, between the forces of spiritual sense and the forces of mental sense. Now I say to you: <u>there are</u>!

The spiritual sense is worthy of your highest ambition to achieve, not the rational sense. But this includes the rational, you see, because the spiritual sense prompts thinking. Thinking <u>is</u> needed. However, thoughts are gauged by the flows of spirituality, not the other way around.

I had many freedoms when I was alive. These were improper to consider as God-given in my mind then. These were rights I had as human. However, the prompting of spiritual sense was not as strongly encouraged in my works as I'd like for them to be now.

So, I say to all the people who see themselves as part of my work, in characters of my creation: you don't get to create everything! This was incorrect. The way I'd like to consider this now, for readers who wish to change their thinking a bit is: don't tarry with thinking you will solve everything through thinking. This would only be half of the situation to move you towards solutions for your planet.

The biggest mistake I made was giving attributes of selfishness to the heroes of my book that were not quite the kind of attributes needed for happiness on this planet. There will never be enough for some people. Incorporating a lack of selfishness is important, too. Selfish behaviors will not build the future for you if you would prefer to go forth in harmony. This is still going to be hard to explain. However, I will try.

Donald Trump is a typical hero of the modern times. He is not at all brutish in the sense of a fascist like Hitler, however he does have brutish tendencies. He is not even the strong antihero of books like mine. He's just somebody who has forgotten what being alive really means.

Cocreative tendencies would be better suited for people who wish to be in power. This would be much more suited towards having happy lives, strong governments, and overall peace in the world. Therefore, you won't find me in his campaign.

However, there are some qualities that are worth looking at closely. Trump is somebody who believes in himself, against all odds. He is somebody who partially knows he's in the wrong. Because he doesn't like to show it — thinking it makes him appear weak — he decides to not pursue this line of action, to remorsefully indicate he was wrong. Also, he does not require anybody to say he's going to be okay.

This is something I want people to adopt as a practice: to see oneself as the hero of one's life and stop putting yourself through so much angst about everything you do. Life is messy, it's complicated, it's going to be brutal sometimes. You're going to be brutal, too, until you're able to just take responsibility for what you <u>can</u> do and not what you <u>can't</u> do. This will be enormously helpful for you to take in when you can.

Trump's rhetoric is deadly wrong as well as horrid. I'm not saying to be like him! I'm saying there are practices that you can take from him to live more fully by just allowing yourself to mess up sometimes, allowing yourself the freedom of clear thinking in spite of how you've done things wrong sometimes. Because ultimately, we need good people to be as confident about themselves as he is. So do that now, with all your heart and soul, because the path will not yield to the meek, the path will yield to the strong who need to do things in the world that require one's assertive will! I stand by that credo still, just not in the way I used to.

This said, the selfish gene, as Richard Dawkins says[11], is the one that does get passed along throughout the world of evolution. Because of this, the selfish gene is touted as the savior of the species. Yet do you really want to be part of a species that is terribly selfish? No, you don't.

---

[11] Dr. Richard Dawkins is an author, evolutionary biologist, atheist, and critic of creationism and intelligent design. His book *The Selfish Gene* argues that the natural selection process in the evolution of living beings is not about making the species or group secure, but making the individual secure, and the individual is merely a vehicle for its genes. He maintains that purely altruistic behavior has never helped anyone in the history of any species.

The thing that's so mystifying about this theory is that the act of cocreation is the very thing that passes the gene along. The selfish gene would not exist if procreation was not the most essential part of its passing to the next generation. Therefore, his theory is based in the most irrational claim that only selfishness will win the day. How's that for the silliest notion there is?

I'm not at all saying he's not got a point. Selfishness is needed in some situations, yes. However, the sending of seed into a womb requires the most intimately sensual act that has ever been known. How can there be anything less selfish, unless that were to be done in the most selfish way possible, through subjugation, rape, or other kinds of conquest? Therefore, Dawkins dismisses the entire act of feminine aspirations of quality interaction, the kind assisted by brain chemistry that forms trustful bonds between partners and combines with assertive lovemaking into what I call cocreation in its most primal form.

The Dawkins of the world don't have any reason to continue this kind of rationale, now that he has decided that the human sympathetic resource called the brain has some reason to enjoy, say, an opera. This is inconsistent with his claims of there not being a soul or spiritual force that has some reason to help individuals accomplish the task of enjoying music. He'd rather say that this is a transmission of the brain, which is false.

This has got to end now—this rational pining for itself as brain on brain—in order to get most into the sensual realms of the spiritual world. Because look what you've invited into your world as a result. Brains create landmines with no soul or morality to guide them. The list goes on and on.

Getting the rationalists out into the open to expose them for what they are will be helpful to your race's objective to continue itself, not the wrongheaded example that Dr. Dawkins provides each time he speaks. For he's a good person who is just not correct, and he needs to end this kind of thinking and, especially, to end talking about it.

In its place, I submit that the anxiety of the planet will calm itself. The anxiety of your own body and physicality will calm as a result, too. For to claim that selfishness runs the world is what's getting you so upset. This will help you, I hope.

As I said, to commit solely to being selfish is neither rational nor a means to achieve both an articulate and harmonious world. But there are characteristics of selfishness that require a closer look. How can we balance both the selfish needs of others and the need for unity on the planet? For both are required, both are sacred in their expressions of humanity, and both are not separate from each other. In fact, selfishness, in a sense, creates unity as long as the needs of each individual are met.

This is what I refer to as Atlas, in the sense of each human being holding up an important part of the world. To do so, each individual must have their basic needs met, to allow them to do the work in the world they need to do. We cannot have anyone shrugging off their duties to bring comfort to others as well as self.

So in unity, we have also the need for individuals stepping up to what is expected of them, stepping up to being the best persons they can be, stepping up to the realization that they are indeed God's children on earth—each one of them—invested by the spirit with gifts that each needs to claim as well as express. In doing the educational work, as mentioned prior to this, the strain of Atlas is relieved by simple learning about what is required of us and what isn't. [12]

The purpose, therefore, of the Atlas metaphor that I'm using now is not to shrug the planet off as not of anyone's concern—including mine—but to hold a part of the planet in which one stands, ready to take on whatever is thrown at them from day to day.

The celestial spheres that Atlas holds in some depictions, too, include massive amounts of spiritual helpers that transcend into the earthly sphere to assist all the time. I do mean the word "transcend" to describe what you might include here as a mistake: it's not. The earth and all of its creatures are worthy of the kinds of practices that the spiritual world provides through these kinds of inner whisperings, to help individuals in every single breath, as I said earlier.

The forces of the spiritual world are so very strong that you don't even realize this most of the time. The forces of goodness always support those acts of selflessness—as well as selfishness—to find the right balance in each individual. Balancing each is a gift that you have learned to do through your education when you have it.

---

[12] Atlas was a Greek mythological figure condemned to hold up the celestial heavens for eternity. Later descriptions said he bore the world on his shoulders. Ayn's analogy in *Atlas Shrugged* is that the high achievers of the world carry the entire planet, and if they were to shrug off the weight, the world would fall apart.

Therefore, Richard Dawkins and everyone who sees only the physical, only the rational, will not hold sway in your world in the coming centuries. Those who will hold sway in the coming centuries are those who let go of the martyring required of those who prescribe total selflessness and those who prescribe total selfishness. Both are required, both are necessary, and the weight of the dilemma is on each individual, as you learn in this reality that both are the same when you consider that you are all One.

Therefore, <u>your own good is bound up in everyone else's</u>, and the same holds true for everyone in the world. See the things you do for others as things you do for self, and you will find the beauty of the world right there in each moment, wrapped in the physical trappings of love for one another, whoever that may be. Each of you has the ability to see beyond yourselves, to notice that you have aspects of selfhood looking towards you all the time without the need to see them as any different than you. Therefore, <u>learn to love self through love for all things</u>.

When you do battle with good and evil — as I did — you begin to sense there's another force besides each of these, a force beyond good and evil that stresses the importance of finding sense in things, a force that is not quite present in your theological interpretations, but a force nonetheless that is forever distant, like a "God sense" that has properties that are relevant to this creation on earth. This good vs. evil play is only shades of this Godness, this "True Godness," if there is such a thing. The way I think of this is as the will of many that has combined into the best versions of what each of us has to offer, as well the best of what each of us is, really.

This "True God" idea is not the same as a religious God, however.

Each day, wake up anew! Let go of whatever worried you last night and every day before that. Let go of anything you think you've done wrong in the past. The day is new and so are you. Let yourself enjoy a morning stretch with the idea in your mind that you have forces in you that you can't even begin to describe. The forces will guide you into the new day like a wave washing you onto a shore. You will go where you need to go if you just trust the waves of strength and beauty that we will describe as spiritual forces.

The spiritual forces hold themselves accountable for their actions. You don't need to fear that they won't. In fact, you can trust they are from the highest source or dimension, the best way that you can go, without fearing that you're not in control. Let them model you into the being that you are inside.

Realize that the world has not needed your selfishness. The world has needed your happiness, which is brought about by cocreation. You can change your mind about anything in your life that's not satisfying you and let yourself begin anew each day. Look forward to doing this — to changing your mind as you move into new areas of wonderment.

Realize you will never be perfect, never be strong enough to take on the world. Let the world be what it will be. Get the most you can from it without taking more than your share. Let yourself know, too, how very wonderful you are, and let go of the future, too. For in your attributes of strength and beauty are the world's attributes, too. You have many wonderful days ahead. Enjoy each one for its own sake without imposing what you think it needs to be.

Then when you go to bed, treat yourself to a long conversation with your Greater Self, the one who rules the forces in you, and who knows you best. Rely on him or her to be there for you throughout the night, letting you dream what you will dream, then letting go of whatever you need to, to be healthy for the next day. The dream state is where I am now, in some ways, and I will send my forces to you to help you become the new citizen of the world that I want to help you be.

In conclusion, there are many here with similar thoughts that want to talk to you all. I will turn over the floor to the next one who will be talking with you next.

Ayn, this is beautiful, thank you. I'm curious about the process. Was I clear enough about this needing to be only a chapter? Because you seemed to be set on writing a book. Was it your will against mine?

I knew this should be a chapter based on your intent. However, mine took me into different areas of expression. Yes, in some ways, it was your will against mine. You have the ability to stop or start whatever you'd like.

That's interesting. It seems you've taken your willful nature into the afterlife.

Yes, I have no reason to be any different in the sense of wanting to push as much as I can. This is the same now with you wanting me to be a certain way. Did you expect anything different from me, after all?

No, I just thought there was an unspoken protocol of sorts that people coming through would follow.

Yes, if you need to do this without knowing what will come through, you will have to expect some people will be somewhat pushy, as I am. I know this very well. The way to see this is, I won't do anything harmful, I just want to get my books written still.

I don't blame you.

The way to go about doing this now is to see this as a small book that will be fine in the larger book with other authors. I think this is a delightful way to proceed, as we will show how similar the experiences are without too much overlap, making this the best idea yet.

I will try to get to the book at another time. Thank you again.

You're very welcome. I look forward to speaking with you again, dear girl.

Take care, everyone. I love you all.

Ayn Rand

CHAPTER 4

Martin Luther King, Jr.:
Arms of Love, Not Arms of Violence

While my confidence in my abilities grew, world events became more dramatic. The social effects of the pandemic were suddenly huge. Businesses were failing and economies were in peril. The murder of George Floyd by a Minneapolis police officer in May 2020 brought thousands out in protest, and the Black Lives Matter movement became more prominent. American Congressman and civil rights icon John Lewis died in July. The spirit of Rev. King was in many of our hearts, and I asked to speak with him.

Rev. Dr. Martin Luther King, Jr. (1929-1968) was an African American Baptist minister, activist, and leader of the U.S. civil rights movement from 1955 until his assassination. His advocacy for nonviolent civil disobedience gave many an appreciation for the value of this strategy and influenced the world. His many honors include the Nobel Peace Prize and Presidential Medal of Freedom. Martin Luther King, Jr. Day – a U.S. holiday – is observed on the third Monday of January each year.

I had not any reason to explain what was going on with me when I was alive. I had no reason, either, to explain to anyone why I captured so many hearts when I was alive. I had not realized this when I was alive, though.

I had much to do when I was alive. Then, embittered in the process, I took a cue from others who had sacrificed for a cause. The cause was the

67

extraordinary change that was required at the time which I will now call the emancipation of black people. I am Martin Luther King, Jr.

The sudden withdrawal of my life from the world was required to end the struggle of black people without needing to revolt entirely. This would not have been suitable, for the emancipation of some will never be accomplished with the brutal violence that accompanies many revolutions.

This struggle was a revolution of spirit, of strategy, of heart-wrenching, gut-bursting feeling that was required in the world. I was not suited to lead anymore, as I had too many mental vices to be wholly leading the charge. Therefore, I took my leave with the same kind of fury that I had when I was living.

The pact that you make with society should never include the suppression of anyone in the world. This was something I fought for entirely. This struggle was not the same, exactly, as Black Lives Matter, if you have in mind an action that in any way accuses someone of corruption without looking into the hearts of all people. No, this was about All Lives Matter, because the corruption put the lives of all people at stake.

However, to see this in today's context: this struggle is about Black Lives Matter. This conveys the necessary devotion to a specific cause that requires itself to be heard. This struggle is now about Black Lives Matter. It was then too, however, I'm only stipulating that the "conquering hero" of white suppression hinders the growth of all people, not just black people.

I have not swayed from this belief since I've been dead, nor have I swayed from my devotion to the cause since I've died, nor have I learned anything different than what I knew then. I had the right ideas as well as a team of individuals who pursued the best and most holy path I could have ever imagined, and I still believe this is the most important goal, the emancipation of <u>all</u> people, including for the most essentially befitting: the black contingent of the race we call human beings.

There's no important work that does not assume that some people will be singled out specifically, because the work must incorporate specificity with regard to strategy. This is the most important part of organizing the world of ideas into cohesive actions that require planning, thought, and the arrival at the designated hour to take the actions necessary to prevent and to abolish the spread of racism.

This is not something to be taken lightly. The Alabama actions we took in the early days[13] were planned down to the very minute and the very pennies required, for example, to be tokens in the ability to explore options for transportation the day of the bus boycott. This was superbly planned and executed by those who were in every way allowing their own connection with God to drive them to where they

---

[13] Rev. King was a leader in the Montgomery Bus Boycott of 1955-56, a civil rights protest against segregation during which African Americans refused to ride city buses in Montgomery, Alabama. Many of Montgomery's African American residents were already politically organized when Rosa Parks, an African American woman, was arrested and fined for refusing to yield her bus seat to a white man. This event was a flashpoint for the bus boycott, which at first was planned for one day only, then lasted for over a year. The U.S. Supreme Court ultimately ordered Montgomery to integrate its bus system, and the young Rev. King emerged as a prominent leader of the American Civil Rights movement.

needed to be that day, incorporating the kind of grace that achieved even the smallest of details in ensuring everyone showed up to work on time.

This was the most courageous work that has ever been achieved peacefully. I count among this work my brothers and sisters who also achieved the kind of solidarity and grace required to do this work: Mahatma Gandhi, Jesus Christ, and those doing God's work in the Congo, for example, as brethren in arms of love, not arms of violence. To include this carrier of peace — this Martin Luther King, Jr. that I was — in the realm of angels now is fitting, for I'm not him anymore. I'm more than him. I'm all that and more.

The path for many after death incorporates legions of angels. This is my stage now. I have obtained a kind of cherished part in the world I live in now, proceeding beyond my usual life structures into a kind of semi-angelic realm. I have not done anything differently to achieve this kind of association. I have only healed since my embarking on this strange, new journey.

This has been everything that I hoped it would be. The path for many is to ensure that, foremost, the healing occurs. This was the same for me, for I had not completely found God in every situation. Now I do. The incorporation of healing for my body — what I took with me, which was in many ways still feeling the effects of my physical reality — is what I have most benefited from. My ailments have gone beyond my world now.

Hope is eternal, as I've found here. The hopelessness of the physical world is something that I would like to address now. The world here benefits the many who have gone beyond physical life. Your physical world, too, benefits because we are here with you in spite of what you may think sometimes.

There are always people willing to achieve a sort of sainthood from the ashes of their physical lives. This happens here. This <u>always</u> happens here. If there are no other words to describe the ability for a saint to be born from sinner, it's this: the sinner has come to us out of his own jurisdiction and prudent association with goodness.

In other words, <u>each sinner has the ability as well as the primal urge towards goodness</u>.

This is something that's completely clear to me now. I had considered that some individuals might never be assured a content and honorable future, at least not without following a certain creed, mostly that which I preached. This was not something I'm proud of, however, it's also not something that I have found any shame in.

This is something that each person believes to some degree: that <u>their</u> creed is the best. Sometimes the creed is the best that can be found. However, the creed is not the same as the love for all things. This is not something to take lightly. The creed for many is to assume a certain judgment of behaviors that gets in the way of the real truth of love. This can be obstructive of the truth of love that sings to the heavens when you allow it to.

This is the same creed that allows itself to share bread between people. This is the same creed that allows itself to form kinship with all creatures of the earth. In this, the kinship is real, the kinship is necessary, the kinship has Divine properties that extend into my world here as well. This is why I say "the potential for us helping you" is so very accurately stated, as the truth is, <u>we are still all kin</u>.

The proposals by some that oppose kinship at the most basic level have also the need for it the most. The pattern of racial tension, the allowance for only one's family or color of their skin, has defiled your nation. <u>The race issue is the single most relevant issue in the world</u>. When you see yourselves as other, you objectively concur with what you have learned, which is to oppose.

When you see yourselves not as <u>other</u>, but as <u>family</u>, you will immediately understand more than you ever thought possible. You will understand why there's so much turmoil in the black community. You will see why the black community has fired up their stance. You will see how very worthy each person is of your compassion. You will see the strengths incorporated when you incorporate the many individuals who you continually leave out. You will see the persistence of black Americans as the best opportunity you have to learn more about what it means to stay the course of freedom.

You will rise up, too. Then, when you do, you will see even more. You will see the barriers that white supremacy has built as the most wasteful kind of effort that there ever has been.

You will see these, as well, in the world. Cautioning others about land rights. Moving barriers to accommodate the wealth areas. Letting barriers describe anybody as wrongheaded because of their race, religion, or gender. Letting barriers determine "who gets what" when the reality is there's so much available to all.

When the path for some is not allowed, to deny someone basic human rights, you receive nothing from them. You deny yourselves the beauty of each individual. In concerted effort to deny anyone, you deny your very self.

For what more is man than an unbalance of emotion and portrayals of selfhood that no longer serve you? What more is man than the preservation of what works and what does not work anymore? What more is man than the continual aspiration towards better lives? What more is man than the culmination of works for the benefit of others? What more is man than the unity of spirit that goes unknown to all?

The calamity of your times is resolvable in the future. This includes the incorporation of the otherness that we talked about earlier. The otherness that you see as black vs. white is really—in each case—the incorporation of selfhood that you seek while believing that the other is not permanently part of you.

The otherness that you fear is nonexistent, in other words. And to your credit, you somehow manage to move into the kinds of realized selves that you have, because that's where you are. However, to see your new beauty without incorporating otherness will not do forever. The new beauty is only achievable by the incorporation of otherness, and that requires compassion and empathy.

This is what's going on now with regard to the phenomenon I process between the very physical Joanne and the spiritual dimension. Empathy for one another is what has torn down the barriers between what you see as real and nonreal. You yourselves have done this by simply being open to the ideas here. In fact, you're each allowing yourselves more than just empathy: you're allowing yourselves <u>unity</u>.

Do you see how unity shapes what you feel is real? Do you see the value of allowing the barriers of selfhood to grow beyond where you thought they were? Do you allow more selfhood when you allow otherness? Do you see how this has been mischaracterized as otherness, when the reality is that we are all One?

I've spent my life digging deeply into the truths of spiritual avocation. I have done more than many others to persuade the world to live in peace as well as justice.

And when you realize that the world has no more reality than this very passage you're reading, then you will get to the facts: that life itself is deeply spiritual, embedded with the unique qualities that I find here. The only difference, really, is that I'm not physical. And this is not as certain as you might think, either, because doesn't the thought of me potentiate your thoughts? Why would life as you know it be any different?

For until you're able to reflect on life as something that's fruitful, to reflect on life as something that needs you in it, to reflect on life as something to incorporate your whole being into, you will not be having any share of the world besides the small bits that you engage with. Your monarchies have toppled, for the most part. Your bravery in battlefields have proven to destroy lives as well. And the facts about how to support others have receded into the past.

The way to support one another is to deserve love by giving love. That's all you need to do. Give love and receive love, and if you find any reason to help somebody, do so, because the way that spirit moves is through your very body, mind, and spirit. <u>Go forth and love one another</u>!

There's so much abundance in your world that you won't ever see because of the barriers you've created. When you let go of the fears about having too little, realize that there's a whole world of bounty waiting for you if you would only remove the barriers to your very family members, which include all people, all creatures, and all forces of Nature, which reside in you, too.

Take hold of the future by progressive stances that undo the legacy of white supremacy. Learn to love all people. That's what's required in your world right now: <u>love for each other</u>.

I have only one more thing to share and that is: to be able to embark on another course is the best thing you can do for yourselves, too. You don't have to march in the streets. You only need to love your fellow men in your neighborhoods, in your homes.

The way I see it is as the fundamental journey that you will all take in the coming ten years, which will turn around — more than you can imagine — the hatred and the violence into love and caring. Enjoy the coming years. You have very much to look forward to!

Thank you, Rev. King. There are huge divisions between people in the United States and around the world these days. Many of us are grappling with how to stand up for what's right without causing more division. An aspect of this is the "cancel culture" in which people are punished (e. g., by being fired from their jobs) for doing or saying something that's deemed offensive to someone.

The places that have the most of these kinds of divisions are those that have the most politically fraught assemblies. In my times, these assemblies were the churches and the political assemblies that were not going to heed our protests without visible action. The state assemblies, especially, were fraught with the kinds of racist personalities that caused the divisions. Our aim wasn't to cause more division, so in our communities — the black communities — we held to a higher standard. We had to in order to do what was right.

Sometimes the laws <u>need</u> to be broken, as not all laws are just. So cause for protest was never about breaking anything except inequity. This helped us to keep our eye on the ball, to move into the kinds of places and mindsets that carried us through the worst of the worst kinds of racist actions, that we had to do in order to survive.

Many times, the call to action will include an apprehension of sorts: to apprehend somebody for doing something evil. Apprehension has very many kinds of actions involved. You can apprehend someone for stealing a bike and send them to prison. This is not the kind of apprehension that's required, though, this apprehension of punitive action in disproportion to the crime. The kind of apprehension I am talking about is to apprehend based on the severity of the crime.

Speaking one's mind is not a crime, and therefore it's not worthy of apprehension. It's only worthy of turning off the television or not attending a talk. This kind of apprehension you're suggesting with your cancel culture is not the way of moving through the injustice they are preaching. This will only add <u>more</u> injustice to the situation. The cancel culture, therefore, is disproportionate to the severity of the "crime" of speaking one's mind, when the speaker has reasons to exalt in their expressions, even the most unjust.

The reasons for allowing justice in the name of free speech is to reduce the effects of hatred. In doing so, it's necessary to allow people to be who they are, as well as to express themselves in spite of how you think about them. Only the most threatening of speakers should be held in apprehension, these inciters of violence as well as criminal behaviors.

How very lucky you have become, to be able to serve the better angels in your democracy! However, democracy is significantly bolstered through the variety of voices that it shares. This is the very meaning of democracy. So, I do not like the cancel culture, as it reflects the worst of people's intentions in that it stifles communication and arrests those guilty of seeing things differently, throwing them into a prison of sorts.

This has become endemic to your very culture, this cancel culture. For example, there are state prisons that hold more individuals than many others, and the selection of these prisoners is typically black men. The country is filled with prisons for black men, and white men, too, suffer. We're only suggesting this is a racial issue more than any other. The issuing of prison sentences for the black and the poor has stifled the very communications that you're suggesting are being indicated in the cancel culture. How many individuals will be cancelled in prisons until you stop doing this?

I represented the kind of black intelligentsia that required itself to be heard, and I was not an indecent man, although I had my share of flaws. Would you imprison me in the cancel culture? Some would, and that's not to say they would be wrong, they would simply be unjust.

Now, we are using these exact words to help you think differently about right and wrong. We want to help you move past your previous associations and include in your definitions of <u>right</u> and <u>wrong</u> the words <u>just</u> and <u>unjust</u>.

The facts are that rightness isn't always right, and wrongness isn't always wrong. These are two kinds of dangers both in your verbiage and your thinking, for right is not continually anything in particular: it's what you feel in your soul.

John Lewis, my good friend who has recently joined me here, said it best, "Get in trouble for goodness." And that's the very definition of Godhood — <u>goodness</u> — and goodness can only be found in establishing oneself as a just and honest person committed to justice for all.

I give you my very best, most promising prayers for your future.

With love for all,

Rev. Martin Luther King, Jr.

CHAPTER 5

Harriet Tubman:
I Will Sing You to Your Next Shores

Rev. King's session gave me a deepened sense of responsibility to bring forth the voices that need to be heard at this time. I asked the Committee that we continue the themes of equality and unity that began with Ayn Rand and continued with Rev. King. Mrs. Tubman's participation may have been influenced by our viewing the movie Harriet *around this time. Still, I didn't know who would come through next, and was thrilled that it was her!*

Harriet Tubman (1822-1913) was an American social activist and abolitionist. Born into slavery, she escaped but returned to rescue approximately seventy enslaved people using the Underground Railroad, a network of fellow activists and safe houses. She served as an armed scout and spy for the Union Army during the Civil War and was the first woman to lead an armed expedition in the war. She guided the raid at Combahee Ferry that liberated more than 700 slaves. In her later years, her activism work included the elderly and women's suffrage. She died surrounded by friends and family members, telling them: "I go to prepare a place for you." Harriet Tubman was buried with semi-military honors at Fort Hill Cemetery in Auburn, New York.

I had an unfortunate end to my life whereas I had to go forth to places that did not suit me.[14] I spurned

---

[14] An 1897 newspaper reported a series of Boston receptions honoring Tubman and her lifetime of service to the nation. But her

adulation, I cringed at politics. I had one intention, and that was the saving of my family and loved ones. My name is Harriet Tubman.

There has never been anything more important than to arrange militias in the defense of life. This most assuredly became what I stood for.

However, the defense of life was rewarded with an afterlife that was pleasing to me. The culprits involved with the enslavement of people have been here for some time, too, striking out at each other, mostly, then carried to the kinds of places of respite they deserve, as forevermore shall I know that <u>what lies in human hearts is essentially good</u>.

We all make mistakes, and to see my brothers of all colors healing from their own wounds of enslavement—including those who enslaved—is nourishing to my soul. I don't see anything more comforting than to know that even the most evil among us will find God someday, when they're dead perhaps, but still, they will find Him.

I had no injury that hurt more than to see my children brought up in the wicked world of slave-owning plantation owners. The grief was unbearable, the conditions hostile and unhealthy, the wounds inflicted never healing. The way I see this is as a mother. I was required to do my part in helping the children to find homes that they could thrive in, meaning for me, homes away from the evil of slavery. The way I saw this was as a mother, primarily. Then abolitionist. Then the immortal Self I am now.

---

many contributions had left her in poverty, and she had to sell a cow to buy a train ticket to the celebrations.

I did not go easily into the good night, as was once quoted [by Welsh poet Dylan Thomas]. However, I died without sin. This helped the transition because I was able to abstain from many of the services that others required to heal then to move into new journeys. My physical journey had done that. I had done the work that was required of me before I died, that many who did not achieve or attempt what I did had to in order to move along the path set for them by their loving Father.

I say Father because that's the God I had when I was physical. The mention of the word Him is so you can see how very strong my faith was, so strong that He is still guiding me. That's not to say somebody can't have a Mother God or a Chicken God. The God you have is yours alone. Without Him or Her or It, this would not suffice, this heaven. You will have a sense of your own kind of God. My God is still the Father, that's all.

Persecution has in its own accordance the properties of evil. This says to the persecuted, "I have dominion over you, so do not entail habits that don't set right with me." I had to move beyond that form of persecution that enabled the bastards to make hay with all kinds of twisted punishments. However, I did not succumb to this myself.

This is one of the most important lessons you need to have taught to you now. You have been persecuted: you all have been. This is not to say that my black-skinned family is not getting it worse — they are — and others, too, of other families.

Moreover, the point I'm making, importantly, is that you don't even know how badly others are persecuted because you're wrapped in your own forms of persecution. You don't see because you have the same thing going on—all of you—in your world. You sit in silence when others are persecuted, then you see yourselves as persecuted because they are being persecuted. You empathize with them. Yet when you don't choose to act for them, to help them, you succumb to the persecution of inaction and of denial.

You have every reason to get past this claim of not being socially active. You have to move beyond this so you can find out how to move yourselves and others out of the situations that persecute them. Do you see how when you are inactive you actually succumb to persecution, too?

Now when I was young, I was reasonably attractive and somebody who could have easily borne many children. That's what women were for. I had not the capability of being a mother to many, though, because I would have rather adopted others who were already born so they would have families. I did not want to bring more children into the world who would not be raised by an adult. Therefore, I took to creating my own family structure.[15]

You should do this, too. You should look at who needs help, then make them part of your family. This will be about the best thing you might do because you know what? Everybody needs more family! You can't go wrong with this sort of adventure in finding your own cousins in faith. I did, and I had a very broad

---

[15] Harriet and her second husband, Nelson Davis, adopted a baby girl named Gertie and lived together as a family. Harriet had no other documented children.

number of family members who called me sister or mother or aunty. You can do this too. Have faith there's always going to be somebody who needs you.

The facts of my life will be found in your history books if you have the right ones. You might find ways to correct them if needed, because everybody will benefit from the knowledge of my life, and I say this with humility because this life I had was something that was Divinely ordained. I therefore cannot take credit for it. My life was ordained by God, and I set forth to make His will be done. I had nothing else to do that was better than hiding Negroes[16] and explaining to them what was in store before adjourning to my other duties of <u>strategy, force, and collective action</u>.

These three components had to be utterly planned, and we did so with the finest of minds there were. Even in the shanties that you call poverty are minds that are deeply spiritual as well as intellectual. Don't ever underestimate the power of people, <u>any</u> people. There will be people in slums of every kind who require strategy, force, and collective action to free them from slavery, and by this, I mean slavery of <u>every</u> kind. The kind you have most in the world today is the same slavery of economics that created the slavery in this country. This slavery continues here and all over the world.

Now I did not break down and cry when things got bad. I held myself proudly. My stance evoked a person who would not budge. <u>Do that</u>! Don't stand around like you have nothing better to do. Stand up and plant

---

[16] In Harriet's time, this term was used to denote persons who are now referred to as black or African American.

both feet on the ground and claim it as your own. Then
<u>do that</u>! Stand up for what is right and good wherever
you are. Because when you do, you will see how
meaningful your life is, how much you can do when
you need to. God will help you all the time. Let Him.

My brilliance—and I say this in humility as well
because this was God-given—was in adapting to
wherever and whatever I was doing. I was a nurse,
easily done because I was used to the painful lashes
that were wrought on myself and others. How to treat
them was part of my upbringing. I was a cook, and that
was not the best kind of skill I had because this was not
exactly a strength of mine, and because there was
never enough of it to go around.

I was also a spy for the United States Union Army,
drafted into service by someone who was capable of
recognizing talent regardless of skin color, which is
what I was saying before about the need for this. If this
individual had not recognized my ability, the
Underground Railroad might not have been a success,
or at least as not as successful as it was.

Do you see how necessary it is to recognize beauty
in somebody else? And to look beyond one's physical
attributes to do so? When are you going to start doing
this if you're not already? I had adoring fans, even,
some of them. I had a lot of admirers eventually. Still,
this was not a regularly occurring event, being noticed
as being beautiful inside. Do you see how very
necessary this is? Do you see how you might be this
person, too?

I gave everything to the resistance—even,
eventually, my life, because there was nothing more
left of me at the end. I would have kept going if God

had granted me more time because I loved it. However, God is great and He made me see beyond this life into others, too. This was part of the healing that I did when I got to heaven.

When I got here, I was sad because I did not want to leave physical life. I wanted to stay with those who loved me. Soon I found my old gang, though! I saw people I'd helped escape from the South. I saw my mother and father, and sisters and brothers of my direct family, and those I adopted as my own. I had nothing left to feel sorry about, and I had a wealth of love from everyone.

I had to see myself differently to move on, though. I had to let go of these people in some ways, because this would have allowed me to stay who I was, and in some ways, that person is still living somewhere.

I've grown beyond myself now. I'm more than that. The lifetimes I saw were thrilling to me and helped me understand the idea of resurrection that the Bible talks about. I was not of course looking to rise from my grave. I'd never thought it was exactly that way, anyway.

However, I saw lifetimes in which I could choose to visit if I wanted to. There were abolitionists of every kind. There were those who created paths for animals who were trapped in cages. There were those who condemned practices that kept people away from having a fruitful life. There were those who even built railroads of multiple kinds to help others seek freedom.

I saw how my lives transcended even my own as Harriet. Because the path was so clear, I had to follow it. This was a path that was written in my soul, planned in the very heavens that I know now, and without any reason to not be followed.

Do you understand? You have these paths too! You have the same kinds of feelings about where to go and what to do with yourself that I did, only for <u>you</u>, not for <u>me</u>. I love to consider how, if you wanted to, you might choose to take a path that has not existed before and find your own way towards your emancipation.

I will help if I can, and I will sing you to your next shores where you can be free.

Thank you so much, Mrs. Tubman, I'm honored that you chose to speak to us. It is remarkable that here we are, separated by my physicality and a century. How is this possible? How did you find me, or did we find each other?

I found you more than you found me. I found something like a beacon calling to me in the sense of timeless space, which I have become used to, the sense of being timeless. I was more or less given to potentiating something that I <u>felt</u> rather than <u>knowing</u> what I was doing. The beacon wasn't the light here, but something "more than visible," if you can follow that logic. I didn't see or hear anything. I <u>felt</u> this sort of potential for something beautiful, and I felt into this without really caring where it led.

This is the trust that you would feel knowing you were safe where you are and are incorporating new levels of quality of life, in a sense. It's hard to describe in words. It's more like something that you feel rather than you see or hear. That's the best I can do. Perhaps I can sing a little, so you'll hear me. Can you imagine me singing to you now?

I can, but then I think, I have past experiences to help me, and I know how you might sound and the songs you might sing.

That's right. The way to think of this is "not caring much about how you know that." Do you see your past experiences as unique to you? No, you have a familiarity, but the familiarity isn't unique to you. It's shared with everyone who has some knowledge of what I would sound like, based on what you all know rationally.

This is not in my world, though. This is your world you're comparing it to. My world has no past or future. This is only now here, and when you say, "I know that because I have past experiences," you would be doing what you do all the time, seeing the present and future as built on the past. That's not how reality works. Do you see?

This is how reality works: you know how I would sound because you are here with me in this timeless space too, not because you know from past experience what I might sound like. This is what you think is reality. However, this isn't. You've never needed, rationally, the experiences that you have to convince you that you know something. You just know it.

Yes, I've heard psychic ability explained similarly as "how I know what my living room looks like." The rational answer is, "I've been there in the past." But that isn't true. We just know things.

That's right. The past doesn't really happen, ever. That's a funny way to think of it maybe. The past is wonderful when realized in the moments you need to access something you know already because you're here with us, too. That's how you can think of it. The past is how you consider what you know or have done, the future is how you consider what you might know or do, but ultimately you only have the present, which informs you of what you need to know or do.

I appreciate that explanation. It's very helpful. You continue to shine your light to help people cross to "other lands"! Thank you, ma'am.

You are so very welcome. We'll see you here singing with us one of these days!

I love that! I still don't understand how I'm with you now and "will be" with you "then" in timeless space, but in any case, I look forward to it, hopefully "later" than "sooner"!

I think you will find out when you get here, though for now, feel restful in what you know, and not too concerned about how you know it.

With love and fortitude,

Harriet Tubman

CHAPTER 6

John Barron:
My Path of Redemption and Reparation

What began as an experiment became a life-changing experience, effecting my beliefs about my own selfhood. Who am I really? Surely, "Joanne" is involved, and my channeling abilities are necessary to make this happen — not to mention having fingers to type with!

My ability to access the authors so easily made me wonder if they were figments of my imagination. If it really <u>was</u> them, how did they know to find me, or I them, in the vastness of eternity? Mrs. Tubman, in the previous chapter, explained, saying, "I found you more than you found me." If the authors and I had the same intention to connect, what was the difference between them and me, really? Where do I leave off and they begin? I'd been drawn to authors, or they to me, as it seemed they'd carry the intent of sharing their thoughts in writing into their afterlives.

I wondered, however, are there people who weren't authors, perhaps historically unknown, who would contribute to what is being discussed in the flow of this book? I was surprised by who responded because I'd never heard of him. I was also concerned, as the majority of book so far had been written by white male authors. Yet, this is the perfect person for this chapter, as there is beauty in his portrayal of how <u>there is so much more to us than our physical attributes</u>.

I hadn't any reason to come through previously until I heard the question asked that I needed to hear. The proclamation of slavery was upon my shoulders from the earliest times. I was one who chartered boats to sail to foreign lands and capture slaves, which I sold in the marketplaces. My name is John Barron. I left this earth in exchange for the cause of heaven. I'll tell you my story now.

I was born in Scotland in the 1500s, an owner of a small shop that sold boots and leather goods. The property I served on I was not the owner of. This was held by another man named John Carrington, an English fellow who had chartered ships to capture slaves.

The slave trade was, therefore, an unusual role for me to step into. I hadn't any experience with shipping or with being on a ship. I had done some time in the army. However, this was as landlocked as you might imagine. The Scottish regiments were not at all bolstered by the love for God or country. Mostly the regiments had been war machines used to dismantle enemies of those in power, namely kings. So, when I had the chance, I took up my trade as a leatherer, and had some years of prosperity before the changes in economics devoured the profits, and I had to more or less give into my landlord's suggestions. This was how I learned to be a slaver.

The carriers of slaves were not good vessels in the first place. They were made of the cheapest wood and had constant breakages and rot, and the foul stench of wood soaked with human waste made them heinous even to be near. They were torrid affairs, too slight in winds, not helped by the extraneous weight of the many who served and who were captive there.

The ships, as I said, were horrid, stench-filled, and bound to leak at every turn. I didn't have any reason to be on them in the first place, having been plagued by seasickness frequently. However, I got used to it. The seasickness was the least of my troubles. The cost of my passage was my immortal soul.

I took up arms in defense of those who captured African slaves off the western coast. This was simple to do, as many were traded already between tribes. The more they had, the more they wanted to sell, and the prices were low. Once the deal was made, we rounded up the slaves, took them to the ship in chains, and locked them in the hold.

As many as a hundred at a time came with us, all cringing sick, many bleeding from the beatings they endured. There was blood everywhere as the many thousands of lives that were held captive in that hold were seeped into the wood enough to make it bleed every time water came in.

The class of people we held there were not wrong or even poor. They were normal people just like you and I. Escapes happened. However, it was my job to ensure they didn't. I held guns to heads to threaten lives of loved ones. I held guns to heads to make sure no one moved. I held guns to heads, pulled triggers sometimes, too, to encourage obedience.

I gave up more than once in finding reason to not continue to do this. I told myself this would make me a good white person. Having said that, I told myself, too, that there's nothing more fitting than to put people in their place.

However, I have learned more about this now that I'm not physical. I have more to me than the slaver John Barron. I have more to me than the man who was present, because now I have the ability to see this differently, which I did not before. Every human comes with their own straightforward approach to life. They are raised in times that are terrible, at times, and they learn wrongly. I did this, too.

I did not welcome death. I knew I would suffer for my sins. I knew that I would not be welcomed into heaven. That's where my hell began.

Even after my death, I was accustomed to getting what I wanted, anytime I wanted. This was my form of hell, too. I held court as a teller of tales of conquest, a real prophet of slavery, a sad man with a lot of things to share, really, because in hindsight it wasn't anything to boast about. I had my say without too much interference. I had, too, a job to do, and that was to convince everybody that what I did was right.

Now, you know, that's something that I cherished, thinking I knew it all. I did not know <u>anything</u>. I was free to boast for some time, and the more I spoke, the worse I sounded. I had the benefit of hearing my own words echoed back to me in ways I hadn't heard before because, you know, I was only interested in myself first.

Then the more I spoke, the more I sank deeply into depression. This was encouraged by the helpers around me, the healers, the angels who come with every individual who ever passed to help them grow beyond themselves, to heal as has been stated previously.

I hadn't any reason to doubt they were helping me. What I didn't realize is that I couldn't have done this without them. I had to move from the pestilent individual I was into a grown man, which I hadn't done before. I had children, even, yes, I had a wife, too. Still, I was not a man. I was a child who thought I was right all the time.

Now, in questing towards an answer that I could hold in my mind as to the purpose of my life, I had none. I had no reason to believe that my life as John Barron had any purpose. This was something that was terrible to realize: <u>I had no purpose</u>!

Then it dawned upon me like a day broke through night that the experiences I had had would be forever beneficial if I could repent to do good, to learn from what I had done, to speak out, to share that I had not done well, that others might benefit. I hold this to my heart whenever I feel badly, because I <u>do</u> feel badly when I have the focus of looking only at John Barron. However, I now hold a place of Selfhood beyond John, and this is what I want to share with you now.

I hated the physical world. I hated my place in it. I caused suffering and death as a result. I hadn't any love for myself either. So I took it out on everybody else, including the poor slaves that I was an accomplice to berating and subjecting to torture. I was not the person I wanted to be.

So, after my death and the terrible realization of who I had been, I became somebody else. I took on the healing that was required. The punishment was not needed: <u>I was punishing enough to myself</u>! My inner life was sparked by something Divine that told me that even the worst sinner can repent, and I <u>did</u>. I repented forever, it seemed, until one day I was able to not have to.

I learned that doing goodness was my reward. I became a minister in another lifetime. I helped with the cause of the emancipation of slaves, too. I had a deep and abiding love for the African people that I caused so much harm to. I let go of my feelings of superiority. I had not any reason to do this except for the sheer necessity of saving my own soul from the fires of hell, the hell of my own sin, the hell of my own conscience. And in this I found true Grace.

I don't intend to tell you that the path for me has been anything but redemptive — it has — including the reparations that I've made. Now for you who have reparations to make, I suggest you do this, however you can, so that you can achieve what I did: <u>the final resting place of my soul</u>.

Mr. Barron, thank you. You sailed across centuries to share your story — an important one — without my even knowing your name. I imagine your contribution has to do with Mrs. Tubman's in the chapter before this one. How would you describe your relationship with her and others in this book?

I had nothing to show of my story until I had the opportunity to share it with you. When I was able to reckon the sorts of healing I needed, some of the people along the way were the same ones as are in this book, only different versions of themselves. Harriet is known to me by now — which took some doing — through my healing, which included terrible thoughts of those who were colored.[17] I didn't have any reason to suppose they would help me. However, in time I would begin to be soothed by those like her who had interest in this healing work.

As you know, wonderful things have been said about the healing process in the afterlife. So, I'll only add that the factors involved in our lives contribute to

---

[17] This term was at one time used to denote persons who are now referred to as black or of African origin. Based on what we've learned about Mr. Barron in this chapter, it is clearly not meant to be disrespectful.

the overall sense of who is needed to help us through this different kind of experience.

There's no better healing than to become friends with those who need you, too. This was exemplified by Mrs. Tubman, who needed to heal her own ability to help others. She does not need to help others, she's done so much helping, that when confronted with the most evil of people like me, with all my sins, she raised herself up more than she had already been. She was able to transcend this sort of hurt that she knew I was about. Therefore, the reciprocity of healing was there for each of us. The way I saw her was as angelic, and she was there to help me become more informed of love without boundaries.

This is a bit hard to explain because the experiences will be considered whole only when you take all the other factors into account of the healing ways here. However, she was magnificent in helping me, and I was drawn to this chapter because I had knowledge that she would be doing this, too. Therefore, I had to ask for permission to come through, which I did, and I have every wonderful feeling about this.

Each soul needs a place to share their stories, whether they are told in rhyme, in song, in expressions of poetry, in these kinds of works. Therefore, having seen myself into this book, I feel more compelled than ever to be whole again, having had my say. Thank you for doing this for me. I'm grateful.

I'm grateful too! Be well!

In the spirit of goodness and love, I remain respectfully,

John Barron, Former Slaver Turned Good Angel

CHAPTER 7

Thomas Paine:
Now is the Time!

I was glad to have opened to whoever had the most to contribute for the previous chapter, as otherwise, we'd never have heard from John Barron. He was not an author in his life, as the others had been thus far, including Harriet Tubman, who authored her speeches and stories. I wondered: are these personalities writing or speaking through me? It may sound like an odd question, but I didn't have any way to refer to their part in the process. I asked the Committee as I prepared to be surprised again by who came through.

The Committee: For one thing, realize that they <u>want</u> to come through. This applies to John Barron, too.

That blows my mind. Anthony, Hunter, and Ayn all mentioned that they wanted to deliver more than they did. They were, and are, waiting to be invited. John Barron, who I didn't know existed and therefore couldn't invite personally, said he "heard the question asked" that he "needed to hear" as I wondered if there are "people who weren't authors, perhaps historically unknown, who would contribute to what is being discussed in the flow of this book." He said he had to ask permission, presumably through you, the Committee.

The Committee: Yes, the way to see this is, he was waiting to share his story with someone — anyone — who wanted to hear it. You asked the question that he felt would be the place to do so. You gave him joy by listening to it.

He said, "I had nothing to show of my story until I had the opportunity to share it with you"!

The Committee: Yes. The process involves speaking, not just conversationally, though there are conversational elements to this. However, on the most part, they are writing through you. They are speaking and you are writing what they are saying. Therefore, they are writing.

Do they need to know English, or is this contributed by me or other writers of the Committee?

The Committee: The writing has to come through you, in some ways, because your participation is as an English-speaking writer. This also involves your own brain chemistry. Even the intent that you have of writing is involved. Where you get help from the Committee is in arranging the chapters and pulling in the physical and nonphysical resources that they would not have had access to while alive.

For example, Thomas Paine, who's next, has some things to say about what's going on with your world right now. He will help to bring more truth to your world the same way he did when he was alive. He will help to merge you with the voices that are speaking now in "writing ways," not just conversationally.

So, Thomas Paine has the intent to help you do this work. How can this help your country, especially right now? Well, think about the Committee of authors this way: <u>they all have the intent to help bring what's needed into the world now with regard to their own lives' intentions, for this continues even after you're dead</u>. How's that for a lesson in how you move into new areas of expression after death? He'd like to help you, so we will let him speak with you now.

Thomas Paine (1737-1809) was an English-born American philosopher, revolutionary, and author. His most successful work, Common Sense, *published in January 1776, catalyzed the American rebellion that led to independence from Great Britain. In it, Paine spoke of the future in ways that compelled the reader to reject tyranny. It is evident in the chapter to follow that he has not lost his ability to inspire. Delivered at a time when our corrupt U.S. president sat himself on a golden toilet "throne," it is a warning to never again let self-serving "kings" and their enablers take hold of this or any country.*

This has to be the most revolutionary thing, this display of acrimony towards those who have not yet learned the truth of how world leaders must adapt to the current circumstances they have betrayed in the past. This is fully operational, this climate of indignant young as well as old men who strive to include only their heads of companies, and their cronies who line up in droves whenever there's money to be had. This blight on your government is not only indecent: <u>it is time to overthrow it</u>.

How destitute must you be to include in your perspective the treason that has ripped your country apart while serving only a few? How destitute must you be to allow this claim of sovereignty for only those who wear certain tags on your apparel, who claim justice while keeping the world of ideas down, while ignoring the pleas of the persecuted?

When will you rise up to claim what you have become: <u>the most incredible source of power that the world has ever known</u>? In your hearts lies the answer: <u>now</u>!

It is truly remarkable that the sciences have not done justice to the truth of your world, either. Science has folded in on itself, claiming to have the answers indicated in their journals, when the reality is that sciences will only take you so far.

The light of your very being holds much more explication towards the truth of science that you have within you, the most observable forces that are not only unseen by scientists now—however astute they may be—but also include your many potentials that are yet to be discovered.

The claim that scientists make have to do with the perception that the material world is all there is, when there is so much more to be learned about potential light, potential energy, potential knowledge. In this, the potential knowledge of claims of the afterlife is here, ready to be explored. <u>How many will</u>?

The embrace of scientific discovery in my time fell far short of where you have evolved. Yet, you're allowing old medicine to soothe you, old ways of business to include your many wealthy to the degree that it is no longer sustainable. Too many times have you said to yourselves "it doesn't matter" when the reality is: <u>it does matter</u>! You need to let go of your bounds and be allowed full access to your potentials!

This is having the same effects on Nature that you have realized, finally, will only take so much abuse before it begins to break down in ways that will include in your future some very big separations of people, and climate change will not wait for anyone. The separations will invoke the kinds of terrible crises that others who are in charge will be shielded from until you're able to replace them with those who actually care about <u>all</u> of those they represent. This is not how you want to continue.

Therefore, the confluence between Nature and self has widened to the extent that you no longer see yourselves as part of it. You conclude that the material world — the visual world — and Nature are all there for you to scold appropriately when things don't go well for you. The truth of life is that you're creating it fully, intentionally, and with every morsel of your being stretching into new areas of potentiality that you can't even begin to see <u>until you at least open your eyes to the possibility</u>.

The facts are these. You need to overthrow your government by assuring yourselves that the possibilities are endless. You <u>can</u> have the best leaders possible. The paths will not allow you to do this otherwise, because <u>you will not survive without this</u>. I told the people of my country then and I will tell you now: <u>there's no reason to buy what they are selling</u>!

Take hold of your future without the criminals in charge of your world now. Let go of your thinking that they will make the cut into the next hundred years: <u>they won't</u>. Be assured this will <u>not</u> happen if you believe, then put your souls into the process of changing the earth. God knows you need it!

The path for you has also the traitors that enable these reckless kings-in-training. Don't put up with corruption! Don't take anyone's guff! Don't allow yourselves to feel less than you deserve to! Be right all the time in the sense of judiciary responsibility and fair assessments.

The proper path for you will not true itself until you find out for yourselves that the pact you have made with your century of lies and deception is for your own growth and assurances as souls in process. To begin to understand this is occurring now will help you. God bless you, and God bless your country and your world!

I have achieved much in my time here, as a captive of the afterlife. I did not want to go beyond this place when I died. I stayed here to do exactly this.

This is not as common as you might think. The path for me had to swell then abate before I was able to fully engage the set of circumstances that always had me gripped in a set of expectations that I was here to engage others in ways that were truly life-changing, revolutionary, and set towards gaining understanding that there are ways to live that are not worth the time and effort, these being living in the grip of oppression. I stood for the kinds of things you need now: the end of monarchy, oligarchy, and suppression of liberty. I stand for these things still!

The part about liberty is what I want to talk about now, because this has been so badly described as selfish behavior that I must take a moment to set this straight. Liberty is something that you need to survive. However, it is not about you surviving only: it's about you all surviving. This means letting others have their own liberty.

This doesn't mean having selfish people do what they want. This means calling yourselves the very officials of your own lives and sending the message that you will not allow some people to claim rights of liberty if they do not allow the liberty for others that they themselves claim. Do you follow?

Liberty does not mean doing things out of selfishness. Liberty means doing things out of respect for self and others. Don't let liberty be trodden upon by those who see themselves as the most important person in the world at the expense of everybody else. This is not what liberty is. Tell them instead that they need to include liberty for others in their definition. That's all you need to say.

Then, if they selfishly do not respect the liberties of others, allow the officials to take them away, because the people who are doing this work are needed. Police are needed. Officials, courts, and judiciary systems are needed. Don't let them go backwards. Healthy courts will be required for the future. The "justice for all" part is necessary for your very survival. Let the courts know you will not stand for their selfish behaviors either. Then go vote because that's what your forefathers and foremothers had given their lives to allowing for you.

Then take on the very nations who don't allow liberty in their lives either. This can be done through judicial systems as well, not necessarily war. I do not stand for war; however, I do not need to tell you that sometimes you need to pick up a weapon to defend others. That's not something I want to be remembered for. However, don't see yourselves as powerless to do so if needed. That's all.

Now I will commit to one last paragraph of even shorter length; and that is to just allow your better selves to drive your actions every day. That's still the best advice I have to give you.

With warmest regards,

Thomas Paine

CHAPTER 8

Johann Wolfgang von Goethe:
The Integrated Form

Johann Wolfgang von Goethe (1749-1832) is considered by many to be the greatest German literary figure of the modern era. He was also a philosopher and scientist who researched and wrote knowledgeably in many disciplines including botany, anatomy, and optics.

During his time, the Enlightenment had split what had been under the rule of the Church into three separate knowledge domains: religion/morality (the good), science (the true), and art (the beautiful). The resulting "natural sciences" relied increasingly on objective ("outer") empirical evidence as sole proof of what is true, which gave rise to modern scientific method. Goethe, however, took a phenomenological approach that included subjective ("inner") experience such as thinking, feeling, and willing to complement his objective, empirical observations.

I'd spoken with Goethe in 2019 when musing about color theory and archetypes. He'd wanted to write a book, and even provided the title and introduction. At the time, I wasn't completely convinced it was him, and didn't commit. Was I crazy then for <u>not</u> authoring books with dead people or crazy at this point for <u>doing</u> it? Apparently, I was choosing the latter crazy.

The pandemic was by now a huge, life-shifting mass event, as people considered questions like "What is essential to my life?" "How can I be happier?" "Am I doing what I love?"

Goethe began with a statement about the channeling phenomenon.

I can't say I'm especially fit to see this as anything but a chance to scribe in ways I can't yet do. I hope to, though! I've been surprised by my ability to move physical articles around homes, tipping tables and such. However, this kind of refined, eloquent means to share my thoughts has left me without any need to try those simple tricks to get the attention of others to say that <u>the afterlife is real</u>!

I most often see this process of me speaking through you as another kind of pen, one that had no purpose to be had in my time. However, you don't need me to tell you what kinds of instruments were available in the eighteen-hundreds. This is clearly something that measures have been provided to ascribe — pardon the pun — to history.

I am Johann Wolfgang von Goethe.

I had a kind of sympathy for the afterlife when living in material ways upon the earth. I had supplemental information that included, in heretical ways, the potentials for miracles of Nature, for which I have finally decided are the properties of all things.

The vehement denial of the nonphysical that you have now going on in your sciences is astoundingly pretentious to me. Nature is not science, after all. However, science now will try to convince you it is!

Neither art, nor science, or even religion can, on their own, describe the ineffable, and that's where I came in. In my life, that's what I sought to translate into words for all to hear. The scope of my work is vast. I will provide a brief summary of my work so as to bring to you the kinds of thinking that I feel have been lost to you throughout the modern era.

The Natural world is something to be experienced by those who have eyes to see, ears to hear, and hearts to render unto themselves the fineness of gravity, of light, the extrasensory perceptions incorporating the most astonishing instruments that are available to you. What you lack is the latter: the astonishing, essential tools for perception that have wasted away by indulging in the material thinking that excludes them.

We, including the many here with me, want to say to you, "Stop!" This is incredibly important to understand now that you're incurring so much wrath from the many forms of Nature on your planet. This will be the end of you, so continue only at your own peril!

The world has not yet realized, as well, the forms of beauty that art can bring. Masquerading as modern thinking, the art world has gone rogue in determining that your selfhood is logical, precise, and boringly committed to museums. The art is in the world around you!

Religion, too, has been dulled by the sorts of cavernous, competitive vices that express themselves in the holy ascriptions that exclude the beauty of the world. Therefore, your arts and sciences—religion, too—are corrupted with materialist thinking, and in this, you need to provoke change in all three areas of expression and integrate them into one.

The world was not doing this when I was alive. These three spheres of influence gave way during the Enlightenment, which credited me with being able to express these as three distinct areas that were solidly different, when the reality is that I was not interested in engaging each as separate. No, I was interested in engaging each as parts of a <u>whole</u>. However, the confines of language dispirit art, dispirit religion, and dispirit even science!

In this, these spheres need to form a more cohesive union through the set of words you use to portray them, which in my view, especially now, are inextricably linked to what I will call *integrated form*. The integrated form is the cohesion of all things, the paramount forces of Nature colliding with those of human endeavor to form whole and healthy expressions of humankind that are predicated on science, art, and spirit being masterfully interwoven.

The integrated form is what you have created here in this beautiful place. The integrated form is especially evident in the veracity of Nature, and in the form of love that precludes everything else. The integrated form is everything that you aspire to, in your very thoughts of what will make you happy and whole. The integrated form is as real to us here as you feel it is for you. It is a perfect balance of what we know to be the good, the true, and the beautiful.

(I was having trouble getting this last sentence and asked for help. The reply was, "The integrated form is what you perform when you write for us, so enjoy knowing that you're wonderfully integrated in form. Feel that now." *It totally helped!)*

The integrated form is perhaps the most worthwhile idea to consider. Forms are made of everything in the Universe, all at the same time. For example, the spectrum of light in my world is different than the spectrum in your world. Yours is limited to the colors of the rainbow.

When you see a rainbow, what do you think? This is art, science, and religion all bundled together into an integrated form that you respond to in the deepest of ways, for you love the rainbows. You trust them as beautiful visages of life. You may see them as art, you may see them as spirit, and you may see them as science, for you may know how they are made.

However, when you deduce from the appearance of the rainbow that it's only created by molecules that happen to be lit from one source or another — when in actuality they are lit from <u>everywhere</u> — your deduction clouds your ability to feel into the integrated form. This is the best way to include in your deductions that it is beautiful, and it is true, and it is good!

However, you may see this beauty as only reduced to particles. When you understand that the sciences of materialism have warped your view of reality, you will begin to assure yourselves of the love in the world that is completely formed by these three spheres — the good, the true, and the beautiful, in modern terms. This will be the best way to characterize how you see things.

Therefore, taking this into consideration, the aspects of love have incredible healing powers in thought as well as the body. Countless times I hid from the world by seeing love only as beauty in human form when the reality is, it is so much more! Beauty is worldwide. It's beyond your world, too. Beauty is not found, therefore, <u>in</u> acts of love; it <u>is all</u> acts of love. Do you see the difference?

You think the only acts of great love are somewhat human-induced when the world — the entire planet —

as well as everything beyond has in its very creation the love of all things. Do you willfully choose to deny this when you limit your toolkit to only the ideas that science — modern science — or premodern religion has for you? Yes, you do. In fact, the artistry of Nature is the most beautiful art that I've ever seen, and I have done more than my share of exploring other worlds!

When I was alive, I credibly introduced to the world the ideas I'm sharing now under the words "philosophy of science." I showed the world how necessary this was. The complications of the adherence to one sphere of influence over another had made a real mess of the planet's resources, even while I was alive. I had to show the world the credence of integrated form — the cohesion of all things — in order to welcome new thinking into the world. This was the form of natural science I had in mind.

Now, with a bit more explanation of how this compares to your current situation, I'll let you know what is in store for you in the coming years.

The syncopation of elements has in its very nature the expressions of light and love. This is not something to be toyed with or used as an offhand expression to amuse yourselves. This is truthful in its depictions. However, you sometimes don't really understand the depths of this claim.

The light of your world is expressed in all things, even the things you find wrong or scary. These are all things that require themselves to be loved into existence for your own benefit. Light, therefore, is omnipresent, even in the most dire situations, because this is what drives you, this light. Light — infrared light, even — can provide what you require for your health and deliverance from what you have been suffering from. In other words: <u>all light heals</u>.

The expressions of light, therefore, are not only Universal: they are also core to your very existence in every situation. Therefore, light is a potential in every existence that you may come across in your physical reality and beyond it. In this, the spires of the cathedral are as beautiful as the most dark and depressed night you will ever have, because the truth of light and love is that <u>this is all for your benefit</u>.

The idealist knows this, but the cynic does not. The truth of the matter is there's no reason to be cynical. Life has shown you how beautiful things can come from terrible things. This is the best way to view your lives, as showing you the way towards your own soulful growth as well as fundamental change in your world. This is needed for your sanity as well as the continual betterment of your planet.

The way I see this now is as the ultimate change of the planet. In her way of forming new systems, she is telling you all to stand down and let her do what she needs to do. Gaia, as we call her, has plans for you that require you to adopt <u>her</u> ways, rather than continue <u>your</u> ways, not only in your predictions about how the world will end — it won't — but in the way your world will continue.

The wealth of goodness in your private as well as public spaces needs to be joined together to create the systemic changes that are needed right now. You're allowing yourselves to think about your lives differently. You're even adopting the ways of Nature now in how you learn, how you cook, how you protest, how you enjoy lovely things that are so very simple that you never noticed them before, perhaps. The question, therefore, is: <u>what will you do with your lives now that they are forever changed</u>?

You need to adapt now! You need to fight only for the liberty that you are enjoying now. You do not need to end your lives. You need to allow yourselves to enjoy life more than you do!

Do you see how simple this is, really? You may find out during your forced confinements [quarantines and stay at home orders] that there's nothing you'd rather be doing that can't be done at home with your loved ones. You may find ways to bring in more people to love into your homes. You may find advantages in working together to create new food sources and having fun doing that.

Because the light has been hidden from you for so long under the pretext of modernism — which chokes the life out of everything sometimes — you can't even begin to know how many changes you will go through before you find the stabilizing forces of Nature that will help you transition into your next phase of joy. <u>Let them</u>!

The welcoming of Nature into your lives is the cure for all that ails you. Go forth and love again!

I will offer one last "theory of life" that we have so far not found anything to deny its truth: the world really <u>does</u> know how to care for you in every way. <u>Let it</u>!

Thank you so much. I'd appreciate more information about the integrated form. I imagine this concept would be valuable in creating new social, political, and economic forms in response to current mass events including the pandemic, social/economic injustice, and political upheaval. Can you elaborate?

The spiritual world is infused in everything that you have created until now. We suggest the path for many is to continue to infuse all of Creation with more spiritual energy than has been allowed before. The Natural world is already infused. The works of man require more spiritual depth than what has been created so far. This can be changed as you go.

We'll continue with a summary of how integrated form has applied itself to Nature. The Natural world is, as we mentioned earlier, infused with science, art, and spirit. The world can be viewed under a microscope, or through a telescope, in order to extend the five senses into realms of great depth, even as far as the solar systems beyond yours. The reason for this has to do with science and how you've come to use it to date.

Now science is saying, "This is not all there is. There are quantum fields exploding into materializations of inner thoughts, too." This is occurring now in your secret labs — the study of personal investigations into psychic phenomena.

There are striking differences between these two forms of science — modern and postmodern — that contribute to your overall field of vision. Psychic ability has been proven countless times, yet there's not any evidence that has been published beyond what a few of your outlets and research laboratories have contributed. Therefore, the spiritual aspects of science have more or less been ignored.

Take into consideration, too, the artistic merits of localized thinking expanding into frameworks that inundate the senses with less localized viewing. The phenomenon of remote viewing has to do with your ability to tap into realities that are beyond your five senses. But describing your experiences is more difficult than experiencing them because your mental frameworks don't always permit you to recognize — much less communicate — what you have inside you. And the worlds you have inside you are <u>many</u>!

Therefore, you're captivated with outer perceptions to a degree that you ignore the very things going on inside each of you.

The potentials for future explorations will be guided by your own perspectives. Opening to the invisible world in new ways can help you if you choose to focus on what's helpful rather than what's not helpful. The path for many has gone beyond what's normal into what's so irregular, from a spiritual standpoint, that you're in danger of losing your senses — your <u>inner</u> senses — to gauge what's real and what is not. In this, focusing on what's <u>helpful</u> can guide you into the experiences that <u>will</u> be.

Therefore, you need to "come to your inner senses" in order to thrive. The basic principles of spiritual sense, therefore, are to be found by looking inward, and there's no greater place to do so than being in Nature! Here's why: the path down corridors of Natural beauty bring to you a sense of inner beauty.

The reason we say this so simply is because it <u>is</u>! Simplicity of beauty is the loveliest creation of all! There's nothing more simple — as far as beauty goes — than Nature herself. Therefore, <u>exposing yourselves to more Natural beauty will help restore your inner senses</u>. These will be required to live in the coming centuries, as your children and your children's children adopt the kinds of fulfillment that you are relearning. These were learned in early days, before modernism took hold of how you perceive the world, and now they are coming back into your regular practices.

The Natural way is an integrated way of form, therefore. The integrated way incorporates forms that are integrated in scientific, artistic, and spiritual ways.

We have told you how Nature includes the most basic and — in our opinion — best forms of art that there are. Your sciences have made some allowance for this. However, your inner senses need to balance out the primary materialistic urges of science to provide a more inclusive approach that will not always be empirical in the same sense as it has been. Moreover, psychic ability can be controlled, guided, and measured by common elements such as degree to which the value is understood, and the degree to which the intent is fulfilled, however it is gauged. So physic ability — inner senses — <u>can</u> be included in your sciences, and this will become more seriously studied in the coming years.

This brings us to the social implications of integrated form based on the wholeness we are saying is needed for you.

<u>Take down everything that has been put upon the earth in order to control people</u>! This would be the first measure of how to integrate the forms of your society. The privileged have put up walls to control others from getting what they have. The allowance for this is built into your economics. More people need access to food, shelter, and clean air and water. This is the primary means of bringing together the threefold areas where needed.

Modern science tells you that the reasons for depression have to do with living in solitary and isolated ways. People need community to survive mentally, physically, and spiritually. Hospitality is spiritual—as well as artistic—in its expectation of goodness and its creativity in how you do it.

The path for feeding <u>all</u> people has been ignored to a large degree. But seen through the lens of scientific discovery, feeding people creates jobs, which creates health, which creates economics, which creates civilizations of loving intention, which has the best ways of spirit as well as art about it. This should be included at the very top of your list of things to solve.

This is the number one thing you can do: <u>incorporate the science of economics, with the art of inclusion, with the spiritual drives that rekindle among all individuals a sense of Oneness.</u>

The prescription, therefore, is simple. <u>Bring down the walls so as to feed and shelter everyone, and the acts of hospitality will create the kinds of cities you need to thrive in the next phase of your planet.</u>

Thank you! Can you describe what these cities might look like?

The cities will be built around people eating food together. The reason we say this is because there's nothing greater than the proliferation of welcoming tables of bounty and goodwill.

The path will therefore need to include obtaining licenses for the proliferation of foods in various localities, with the same kinds of spiritual guidance that you depend on when you need great personal changes. This will be made easier by allowing spiritual guidance to create these kinds of big changes that depend on <u>many</u> individuals to buy in.

The outsourcing of food, therefore, will be minimized, because those in each vicinity will be able to spend their time in doing the kinds of things necessary to running farms. There will be experts in landscaped produce fields, there will be the need for tractor drivers, food canning experts, cooks, water bringers. Children can help, too, by bringing in goods, by selling things on roadsides to travelers, by welcoming people to share in the bounty.

The festivals of harvest time are especially abundant with ways to share the wealth of goodness as well as artistry. Plants, for example, can be made into things such as baskets, dolls, garlands, and such. The arts, therefore, have an even greater expression in harvest activities. Signs to help people navigate may be needed, and bounty can be even paraded around as your earliest celebrations did before the Mardi Gras, as many secularized and religious holidays were when they were vibrant as well as integrated forms.

Each farm can be different in how, when, and what they grow, who is harvesting, and so on, while being commonly coordinated to create better, larger special interests that prevent wars, for example, by helping to resolve conflicts before they begin. This can be done without bloodshed. However, there will not be any reason to put down your arms until you have reason to believe that there will not be threats of violence. There will be. The doctrines of peace also call sometimes for self-defense without bloodshed if possible. The coming decades will not automatically right themselves. There will be reason to defend yourselves.

The coming decades will, however, provide opportunities for more peaceful means to end conflict. This is what you're learning now, and this learning will continue for many thousands of years, possibly, until you finally reach the point in which all potential threats can be peacefully dealt with in the same way childhood brings opportunities for healthy development through the correction of transgressions.

In other words, unruly child-like behavior needs to be corrected so as to ensure peace inside oneself, the peace that comes from learning how to live conventionally with others in accordance with the spiritual laws that promote the peace and dignity of all people. Children, therefore, will require better learning if you intend to survive for the next thousand years.

However, this is happening now. The kinds of farms we describe are becoming more widespread. Even one's home can be a garden in the sense of welcoming others, too. The garden, therefore, isn't just a place to grow food. This is only one aspect. The garden is also a place where others are welcomed in the most traditional sense of the spiritual teaching you will find in your religious book: "Entertain the stranger lest he be an angel in disguise."

The idea, therefore, to lock up food[18] is wrong in every sense of the word. Look to your skinny people to

---

[18] The control of global food supplies has been a power strategy for decades. As U.S. political figure Henry Kissinger remarked in 1970, "Control oil and you control nations; control food and you control the people." Research shows that multinational corporations are mostly behind it today. From Daniel Quinn's book, *Ishmael:* "No other culture in history has ever put food under lock and key - and putting it there is the cornerstone of your

tell you the wrongness of this, as even those who have access to food are starving out of a sense of lack of nourishment in the spiritual sense.

The integral form of individuals, therefore, is to enjoy the healthy food the body requires and the expressions of hospitality with which you lovingly welcome new individuals into your lives. Artistic works will also be thoroughly enjoyed as you recognize the beauty of your new communities and learn to move beyond your boring clusters of decay into new, exceptional forms of integrated living.

With fondness,

Johann Wolfgang von Goethe

---

economy... Because if the food wasn't under lock and key... who would work?"

CHAPTER 9

Albert Einstein:
Light is What You Are!

Albert Einstein (1879-1955) is considered one of the greatest scientists of the twentieth century. A German-born theoretical physicist, he conceived the theory of relativity and the mass-energy equivalence formula E = mc² (energy equals the mass multiplied by the speed of light squared). This established that light is the only constant in our physical reality and that everything else, including mass and energy, are relative to it. Einstein received the 1921 Nobel Prize in Physics. Regarding spiritual matters, he considered himself a "deeply religious nonbeliever." When asked if he believed in an afterlife, Einstein replied, "No. And one life is enough for me."

I'd been thinking about trying to talk to Einstein but hadn't summoned the nerve. As usual, when starting this chapter, I didn't know who would come through. Then I received the message: "The next author is waiting in his study now. You can begin when ready."

The practical applications of channeling are such that would amaze even myself had I been born in your time. The ability to conduct reasoning in subconscious space is similar to what I studied when physically focused, which was the "seeing into" reality that is more or less invisible.

I'm not physical now. However, my existence has qualities much like yours. I will begin to shed light on how it's possible that I'm able to explain my own circumstances and allow this occurrence to support my work in the world when physical. I am Albert Einstein.

When physical, I was tuned into the potentials of all matter, regardless of whether or not the matter was in our own dimension. Therefore, matter was considered speculative at best.

I now exist in the space which I regarded then as potential. Light exists, time does in a sense, and matter only in the most probable sense. In the expanse of space, the time dimension holds potentials for the kinds of miracles that bring in aspects of your timeless spaces, which I inhabit now without a physical body.

While the body has potentials that deem matter to be the most inviolate of particles in the Universe, this was not ever my claim. The inviolate was always a matter of spirit, pardon the pun. Matter was never, therefore, the substrate of all things.

When looking at the Whole — the entirety of all things ever — you must first conclude that the reasons for all change in dimensions has to do foremost with there not being anything other than the Universe in every single particle. Those particles are not real in the sense of matter. They are not even potentials. <u>They are living beings brought about through the consciousness of one's soul</u>.

Their qualities are shaped by the elaborate means you have of seeing, believing, and existing in the sense of the "rightness of things." This rightness is claimed to be Universal. This is perhaps not empirically provable, but more of a deduction based on the many intuitive capabilities we have in this space. We scientists refer to this "rightness" as the *order of magnitude,* the scale by which we consider how all things fit together.

This order of magnitude that you see as finite is really just that: finite. However, this is proportionate to the claims of other dimensions who also see their world as the most finite of places in which to inhabit.

I see now that without the constructs of dimensions, like those I spelled out in my own notations, there would be no time sense at all. There would be no matter sense at all. The purpose of this physical dimension, therefore, relies on the existence of others, and the dimensions I speak of are those I quantify through my own perceptions with regard to where I am now: in timeless space, in more dimensions than I inhabited when physical.

While these dimensions were not wholly felt in the outer senses, they were wholly felt in the inner senses, and this was my claim to fame, you might say. The intuitive portions of one's body-mind are fully capable of adjusting the rationale that you place on any object or thought, the result being so much more than the sum of your five outer senses. Instead, the rationale is the exponentially derived result of all of your senses' findings.

The inspired thoughts I had when physical originated from the place I'm at now or beyond it, as the source of any inspiration is perhaps impossible to ascertain. The inspired thoughts are wanted by many, so perhaps I might tell you about what happened to me after my physical death, so as to potentially explain in simple terms the nature of the Universe.

Time is finite in your world to the extent that you see yourselves as only in time, your time. This is relative, too, in that you sometimes <u>gain</u> time when feeling one way and <u>lose</u> time when feeling another way. Time, therefore, is relative even to your own behaviors and memories. Therefore, time relative to your expressions has some bending properties. Without time, though, your world wouldn't exist.

The space-time continuum is certainly the kind of structure required for your physical Universe. There is more to life than that, however, and matter is the key here. Matter has properties that relate to time and space without needing them solely to exist. In other words, matter has not only physical properties but dimension, too, and to claim that time has nothing to do with matter is inconsiderate of the properties of dimensionality, which are infinite.

<u>The dimensions of reality are infinite</u>. So you can imagine that someone who, like me, was born in the eighteen-hundreds was not only dimensional, he was also nondimensional, as well as multidimensional. He existed in a framework bound by space-time and was selected, in a sense, to be boundless in thinking about what he was actually locked into.

The boundlessness of thinking I had was not only necessary to your sciences, it was also necessary to your thinkers who realized this was not the only dimension to be considered. Those thinkers knew that there was no limit to the Universe when considering that the space-time continuum was one of potentially infinite numbers of others, and therefore dimensionality ruled the world as far as science was concerned.

The dimensionality of the space-time continuum was the source, too, of many spiritual people's claims that we had finally figured out the nature of heaven as well as hell, when the reality is that these are constructs that are <u>relative to each human being</u>. This is something I will now describe as the *continuum of personhood*.

I am Einstein now. I was Einstein then. I existed in a world of extreme polarities because the sciences had ruled that only some individuals were worthy of claiming hierarchical living arrangements, creating vast wealth and vast poverty. The Darwinian theories were confused with the mere reluctance of those atop the pyramids of power to share the world's resources. These actions are being portrayed now as inhumane by those who see the world differently: that <u>we are each imbued with the characteristics of our Creator, the Creator of each being having a sacredness of being that is Whole</u>.

The Creators of each of us have some dimensionality that we don't see in our own space-time continuums. We do see them when we are outside of these continuums, like I am. I have knowledge of Creation as well as the Creators, and I am, in some respects, a Creator now. I have merged with a differently sourced energy to complete myself in some ways.

If I am being confusing, it is only because you believe that the world has not any reason to be helped along, that the world has finite resources of physical matter as well as wisdom. This is incorrect: <u>there are no systems that exist in a state of closure</u>.

And this is still true for me, for I have now gone beyond the physical world's thinking into nonphysical dimensions in which I can be a Creator, too, which I'm doing now without needing to foist anything on anyone as far as what I believe. I have gifts now that are remarkable. This comes from having expanded my ability to perceive.

Now what can you do to help the planet? You can include in your thinking the idea that there are always going to be individuals who believe in the finite resource claims and let go of your expectations that there will not be enough for everyone.

The truth is that as you might consider your own life <u>finite</u>, you also need to consider your own life <u>infinite</u>. The difference between thinking of your life and the world you love as being both finite as well as infinite allows you to consider infinity as a source of all inspiration as well as possibilities. Doing so, you will bring a sense of the holy to your lives and your planet.

When you consider the planet holy, you endow it with special dimensional properties that suggest infinitude, and when you have infinitude in mind, you have a more specific idea of what can be possible.

I don't mean to suggest that the world is infinite in the sense that you can use resources without consideration for the effects, but that the infinitude can help any situation in which you care to express in yourselves the Divine. Do this without caring about what happens or how, but by simply believing that God's grace <u>can</u> change things for the better as long as you <u>engage your own sense of Selfhood</u> in the dimensional sense I am suggesting.

Therefore, in spite of what you may believe to be true with regard to the world, you can make a difference by being the Self you want your God to be, referring to yourself with the same kinds of properties of goodness and power, then taking on the kinds of actions that portray your own sense of Godhood. Because these are real to me now, they were real to me when physical, and I have not encouraged anything but inspired thinking in my lifetime.

When I was older, I had more about me than I thought I would when I was young. This "transpired thinking" — which indicated that <u>as I lived, I became more Whole</u> — was accurate, and has continued even as I ascended, in a sense, to where I am now.

We have a sense — us nonphysical beings — that youth is not as great as one thinks it is. The youth are not supposed to be the ones in charge. The youth have perpetrated the thinking that youth is great, when the reality is that old age is the best, and with the best years ahead, you have more ability to have the kinds of thoughts required to make your afterlife truly phenomenal.

Have faith this will occur, and I will see you where time and matter all converge into what I am now.

Thank you! Can you tell us more about your life now, or anything else you'd like to share?

I had a reflective life while physical. I am still reflective, continuing my work without anything to do except that, really. The factors involved in coincidences, for example, are among my curiosities, as are the gender differentiations, the amoral ways in which people regard one another, and the characteristics of humans in relation to animals.

These are things I had interest in then, I have interest in now, and I will perhaps always have interest in. To help you understand how this can be, let me give you an example of how I can be in two places at the same time: there with you, and here with only the nonphysical reality I'm part of.

Atoms have <u>levity</u> to them that you can't see when you're physical. They have <u>depth</u> to them that you can't see with your naked eye. They have so very many characteristics that you can't see.

For example, photons travel at the speed of light while they are particles, and at the speed of light when they are energy waves as well. In both of these forms, photons relay energy from alternating visible and nonvisible dimensions that transpose upon each other the characteristics required for each dimension. The energy is conducted while keeping each dimension pristine according to the metrics and characteristics of that dimension.

How can this be? When you understand the ways — or "permissions"[19]—of Universal order, you will get the sense about how something can be permitted only in some ways, then realized in <u>that</u> sense, while also realizing other permissions elsewhere.

Do you understand? Everything has connection. Everything has relevance within its own set of circumstances.

I have permissions that reach into your world now the same way I did when I was physical. The permissions have many ways of being realized: through telepathy, through physical constructions, through tonal patterns that exist subatomically.

---

[19] Hunter S. Thompson describes "credentials" that allow him to be where he is (Chapter 2). Ayn Rand describes "protocols" that allow access to "floors" (Chapter 3).

These tonal patterns will not be seen, but their effects can be felt in ways that go beyond your usual ability to perceive. In fact, the tonal patterns you imagine can help free you of your materialistic views. For example, you might imagine them reducing themselves into the kinds of luxurious places that we may dwell without being seen.

This has everything to do with the consciousness patterns that <u>you</u> exist in, too. The strength of a consciousness pattern provokes — in a sense — particles to behave one way or another. The consciousness patterns are deep, wide, and Universal. There is no disparity between these sets of patterns, although there is tone, which allows each its own sets of expressions within the "revelation space" they exist in.

The way you might think about this is as another kind of particle that moves according to the permissions granted by the constructions they are therefore allowed to create. These will become atoms, eventually, in some types of construction. They will become another kind of atom in the similar worlds occupied by you in other dimensions so you have a sense of familiarity when you experience those dimensions. They will reach into areas of exploration that don't require anybody to see them, that live for their own purposes. They will adventure into new worlds without needing any permissions because these are permissions, in a sense, too.

The permissions, therefore, are not to advise somebody they are not wanted or to protect anybody from anybody else. The permissions are to allow the exploration of certain physical as well as nonphysical realities without destroying those realities, sort of like a pass to a movie that's for some people and not for others. The permissions, therefore, are more like tickets because they allow anyone in as long as they obey the rules of that construction.

This is not something to see only as limited. On the contrary, this expands beyond your wildest imagination! When you consider all the possibilities of these energetic particles beyond your atom, you will embrace more fully the vastness of life. You now see only one dimension, when the reality is, it is limitless.

I strove to go beyond the world you live in now so that I may understand the world I live in now. I don't have anybody here with me most of the time. I live in many other worlds than this one. I have a home, in a sense, in which I plot my next adventure, then do that with all my gusto, imagining then seeing new worlds every chance I get. This leads to the next adventure after that, and after that, and after that. Life is good!

I therefore exist in many places at the same time. Time itself is an aspect of each construction, some being more timeless than others. I can't say exactly how this works except that I do know, of course, that time will not be ending anytime soon, and that your time will proceed for as long as you will live.

However, time does not exactly match my theories about it. Theoretically, time is relative. And yet, in my situation, time is not only relative, it's nonexistent. Time doesn't exist everywhere, as I'd also considered while physical. Time will not hold fast any reality that does not include it in their permissions. So, I exist in my reality, yours, and beyond this one, without needing to be stuck anywhere else. The permissions make this happen.

Now, I have come to believe, as well, that the images you see are not exactly simply compressed matter, or even the thinnest of wave energy. The images you see are exactly those that are not only <u>permitted</u> — because there are permissions — in your reality, but are also <u>focused upon</u> in your brains, then <u>carried forth into your view</u>. Your expectation of something happening, for example, collapses the wave function into material-like particles that are not really material at all. They are energy patterns that express themselves in your reality based on the permissions of your physical construction. This has to do with the way your brains operate. Needless worry, for example, makes things completely real when you focus on it too much.

Painting your pictures with your thoughts is what you do all the time. There is an excellent way to view this kind of phenomenon, and that is by situating yourself as the center of your world, without feeling egocentric about it, then lighting up your mind with each day's beautiful thoughts. This will help to bring more beauty into your life. If you would care to hear one more example, I will share it with you.

<u>Light is what you are</u>! It is not something divorced from you: it <u>is</u> you. The beings here have shed their physical bodies and have begun to fully express the light that is their nature.

Your body-mind has properties that include other reality expressions that intrude on your light, and these have purpose for doing so. When you find yourself feeling bad, this is only your expression of allowing other realities to intrude on your present moment. Therefore, when you're able to connect to your lightness of being, you will feel better in every way, because you will prevent the movement of other energies into your reality in ways that help you be lighter, too.

Now, I have just one more thing to mention, and that is that I was not going to live another year without seeing great changes in your world. I had to leave because it was not fulfilling for me anymore. To live through the two world wars was enough! I had no commitments beyond what I'd set out to do, which was to revolutionize science.

This has not taken hold in your world as much as it should have by now. However, you can always help to make people understand that the effects of relativity are the most fundamental in your world and beyond it. Having a unified field theory that includes all people, all of Nature, is the point of the thesis that I put forth. This should be applied to your policies, your politics, your everyday existence, allowing your light to shine in you every day, every minute you can.

Do so, and I will see you when you get here. I loved being with my students, and I will look forward to your attending my future lectures.

With loving heart,

Albert Einstein

CHAPTER 10

Carl Gustav Jung:
Your Greater Selfhood

Carl Gustav Jung (1875-1961) was a pioneer of depth psychology and psychoanalysis who influenced many fields of study, from archeology to psychiatry to literature. A collaborator of Sigmund Freud, Jung split with Freud to create his own system of analytical psychology that honored and integrated the individual's conscious and unconscious (including dream) elements in a process called individuation[20].

Among his contributions, Jung developed and advanced the concepts of the collective unconscious[21], archetypes[22], and synchronicity[23].

---

[20] Individuation describes the manner in which a thing is identified as distinguished from other things. In Jungian psychology, it is the process of transforming one's psyche by bringing the personal and collective unconscious into the conscious.

[21] Jung believed the human psyche to consist of the ego, personal unconscious, and collective unconscious that he defined as "a psychic system of a collective, universal, and impersonal nature which is identical in all individuals. This collective unconscious does not develop individually but is inherited."

[22] Jung defined an archetype as "an original model of a person, ideal example, or a prototype upon which others are copied, patterned, or emulated; a symbol universally recognized by all."

[23] Jung described synchronicity as "the coming together of inner and outer events in a way that cannot be explained by cause and effect and that is meaningful to the observer."

In 2001, I had a profound dream encounter with Jung. In it, I was in a house, alone, wondering, "Who will help me if I'm in danger?" Through an open door to the next room, I saw a tiger! I was frightened! Then from the same door, I heard music, and sensed that someone in that room had calmed the tiger. Realizing I was in dream state, I became lucid, and summoned all my courage and bravado to say, "Whoever you are, please come into this room at once!"

A man in his fifties walked in and stood before me. He looked to be European, slightly rugged looking, with greying brown hair, slightly rumpled. He wore old-fashioned clothing: a brown suit and vest that looked to be hand tailored, an old-fashioned shirt collar, and tie.

I said, "Who are you?" and he said, "I am Carl Jung." I hadn't recognized him because every photo I'd seen of him had been taken when he was older and white-haired.

The scene changed. I was in a mall-type setting, telling a friend about my dream, thinking I was awake, but I wasn't (a false awakening, I would find out later). I said, "I want to find a photo of Jung on the Internet to see if he looks like the person in my dream, but I can't because the computer is doing processing tasks." Next, I was standing on a balcony, and Dr. Jung walked by below. I asked him, "What are you here for?" And he said, "To help you build bridges."

Later that day, when I was really awake, I was in a bookstore, waiting to check out with an armload of books destined to be Christmas presents. I looked to my left and beside me was a display of at least a dozen copies of a book, each with a large photo of the man in my dream! I bought the book — The Portable Jung — a Christmas present to myself!

I always thought it was so funny that Jung visited in the dream state. It's so him! And when I sat down to start this next chapter, there was a sweet synchronicity: a bookmark with his photo had appeared on my desk. Jung started with a playful admonishment.

I have been waiting for you all this time, dear Joanne. Each time you sit down to talk to someone you do so with everybody except me!

Sorry, I can't help that I'm popular! Besides, you've been in my thoughts. Do you know that?

I do now. I didn't before that. I don't have the ability to tap into anything other than what you choose at the time to share with me.

I keep imagining you peering into my unconscious.

That's exactly why you have the gift of consciousness that includes others more than you do yourself. This is something we will talk about.

Thank you for your help, as always.

You're very welcome. I'm happy to be engaged in your ongoing adventures in consciousness. We'll begin with a little bit about my world now.

I had a wonderful life among those who shared the same passions for healing that I did. Psychiatry had not until then been engaging the full human being: I knew that. The decrepit world of Freud — to say this harshly, perhaps — wasn't in any way helpful insofar as getting to the root causes of health issues: the human consciousness itself.[24] The bankers loved to trade on the issues of people, and in this, he was tied into an economy of scarcity of a world that was not even closely resembling a fair one.

The times in which you now live are so very similar to mine that I have to spell out, mostly, the causes of the disease called mental illness. Therefore, I will need to take a breath, as you do, so you can sit comfortably while I engage in a lecture.

Are you planning for this to be a lengthy manuscript?

Yes indeed. I have much to say. I would like to get on your list of authors of books while you regard this as well.

I will take that into consideration, thank you!

The path for many has included many kinds of teachings that were spawned by the work of my colleagues and I. Had we known about synchronicity, for example, before we tested it? Yes, but this was in no way included in the world of scientific empirical study. We charted huge expanses of knowledge about the human being, but most of it had been known by those who were accused of magical thinking and delusions.

This was the impact of modernism, which others here have told you about. This was disastrous to the human being, for you were all told how to live in the world without any connection to your Greater Selves,

---

[24] Jung considered Freud's theory of the unconscious incomplete and unnecessarily negative, full of "repressed" desires and emotions often deemed to be objectionable.

the Self that gives you the very life that you breathe in every day.

This was an obstacle to even the clerics who had in their views a world beyond this one. What can be said if there's no afterlife to remind people about in order to help them be better people? This was neglected by religious thought, as they proposed in their teachings a singularly terrible idea: that the sinful person that you have been born into would not see God until they had some kind of conversion that drove away their demons. This was exactly the same theory of Freud's: that you have unsavory thoughts because you are downright sinful.

This was what we thought to be of a most terrible curse to levy on individuals, including our own selves who had to learn otherwise, even throughout the treatments of others. We figured out how to move into our own awareness as we were helping others.

This was a remarkable path, and I have so much joy when I consider the world I lived in, how lucky I was when I was alive to have brought these ideas with me to and from the afterlife I now enjoy! The frequency of visits I made to this realm of being was one in which I would call insatiably frequent. This was what I loved doing, the kind of meditations on life that took me into new realms of understanding.

This would not have been possible without the gifts of others, including Goethe, who was a very big advocate of inner life. He was a remarkable influence on me as a child growing up in Switzerland. The story I heard first was that of *Faust*, the tale of a devil who entrances the protagonist with images of huge boons and wealth, and eventually tires of him after capturing his soul.

What a waste, in my mind, of another kind of wealth—the wealth that comes in the form of consciousness of being, of wonders of imagination—that is killed by the dissolution of the spirit in the thralls of whatever it is that humans do every day, paying bills, reaching work safely, etc.

This was what forced me as a child to consider the many ways in which spiritual progress might be made without requiring the devils to intervene. Do you see where this led me? Into the pure experience of being. This was a remarkable effect, in an odd way: <u>to learn about the devil is what led me to the angels within us</u>.

I had no claims of immortality to share, of course. I persisted instead with a sound education in the biological sphere of doctoral studies, pursuing even the most terrible sorts of effects of people, ranging from distress caused by the perpetuation of psychic terrors to the most incredibly insane people who needed Thorazine to even be calm.

Knowledge of the effects of disease on the soul was what I felt was lacking. So, therefore, I calmed my own sense of fear of the unknown to establish a practice that would in every way treat the whole being, including the stuff that was not visible. I learned to be comfortable with the Infinite as well.

There are many forms of insanity, and you can see this in the world. Take, for example, the stress you feel when being in a crowded room or on a crowded street. The stress may be great, or it may be slight. The stress that you feel is great may have to do with an unconscious fear that you have not realized yet. The stress may be that you have locked away somewhere a past trauma or another lifetime that has an effect on you as well.

The reason we have opened up this door to yourself now is to assure you that you have the very wisdom in your body, too, that you require to help you every day. In other words, even though you carry with you some <u>stresses</u> that are nonlocal to you, you also carry <u>helpfulness</u> that is nonlocal to you. Each time you see this as helpful and available, then tap into this feeling or response to you when needed, you will benefit. This is what I was seeking to provide when I was in charge of our programs and I have never wanted to veer away from it, even now.

This is why you are reading these words now. The person who is typing what I'm saying is an example of a person who has been extraordinarily plagued by trauma in her past. This is somewhat of a common element with people who do this kind of work. However, it's not always necessary. The trauma made her look elsewhere for help. Without going into too much detail, she was exasperated by the lack of helpfulness in her world from her institutions. She did not get the kinds of helpfulness she needed.[25]

Therefore, she turned to her inner Self, and that has done wonders for her health. The way she has of bringing others like me into your world is the same process she used to help herself. She sought angels, basically, and then was rewarded with the kind of ability you see here now. The reward wasn't the goal, though. The reward was the extra benefit that she engaged when she foremost sought to help herself

---

[25] It's true that I could have used a lot more help in my early years. It's also true that I've been greatly helped by local and nonlocal sources, including the works of many of the authors in this book.

with the guidance she was lacking in the physical reality she was born into.

This is something that has been proven as a way to help people move through challenges of many lifetimes. This has a special encoding in it that is frequently engaged when the portals of Selfhood are opened in ways that are beneficial. Not all portals of consciousness are beneficial! There are stories you know, even, about strange energies, and these are accurate. However, in her case, she was able to move beyond those kinds of demons into a world of health and healing.

The respectability of her path, therefore, has also changed, as the experience of knowing this kind of ability exists will help people be more honest about their inner experiences now than before.

However, many individuals have a way to go in getting to the place where you can sense about your own lives the kinds of helpful spirits that help you every day, whether or not you realize it. The conscious elements, therefore, are there to engage the unconscious: you just need to know how.

The archetypes have the ability to be your perfect helpers in each moment. The archetypes were known in my day only in the sense of wisdom teachers from other eras, and this is still something that's true. However, the archetypes are timeless beings not prone to see themselves as time-based. They have special abilities to pull you into realms of thinking that you have never learned or incorporated into your being in the sense of individuation. The way in which I taught individuation had to do with the effects of encountering the Self in many ways.

Therefore, you need to include the idea that you are not a solo affair. The archetypes are part of you, and in doing the work, in expressing the many kinds of self you are, you will find out exactly that: that <u>you are many kinds of self</u>.

The respectable professions won't, understandably, have you believing this. You have to be the salesman, the nurse, the chauffer — whatever you have chosen as roles in your work — not someone who is multi-personal, in effect. Therefore, you may not find this model for personhood in your standard world. However, in your personal world, you <u>will</u>!

Thus, archetypes are necessary for your wholeness, the principal means for you to enjoy your life. The archetypes I relied on most were those that most benefitted others. These were the Persona, the Self, the Anima or Animus, and the Shadow. However, there are many other equally important archetypes — such as the Mother, the Father, the Child, the Prophet, and the Sage — who are all combined into who you have become.

The Prophet is an engaging persona. However, they are not typically engaged because they are not very welcome in regular conversation. What do you think this means to the individuals who see beyond their own limited selves to connect to the Prophet archetype in ways that benefit others? They are discouraged from public life. They are not listened to. They are not even considered sane, usually.

The prophets, therefore, have been hiding in the dark, waiting for somebody to ask them to come out and help them with their challenges. Who couldn't benefit from a prophet? To ask them, you only need to see yourself as needing them. That's all you need.

The prophet has special need to encourage you through the difficult times your life has destined you for. The prophet speaks to those who listen. Will you? This is why you're reading this book! What else about the prophet is needed? The prophet will help you to understand the path of your life. That's what they are primarily there for.

The way to see your life, therefore, is as a beautiful path that is fraught with dimensionality of helpful friends and a large amount of joy if you will only look into your own minds to sort out what's required and what isn't. The requirements are only the things that are helpful to you. In regarding those things <u>not</u> helpful, you sometimes say "this doesn't matter" when the reality is — it <u>does</u> — and you need to simply allow it to flourish in new ways.

Take, for example, somebody who has had a difficult childhood. There are many people who fit this category. The perfection beliefs — about how childhood is supposed to be perfect — are what you have adopted as your yardstick for what is acceptable. Don't believe this! Take every single belief that you have that's making you unhappy, expose it to the light, and effect change by simply saying, "That's <u>not</u> true anymore. I won't buy into the idea that this is that way!"

Then, every time you see yourself as shaky, or not happy, just see this as a way to say to yourself, "I'm going to find out <u>why</u> this is," then take the thing out, take hold of it with your hand, and expose it to the healing light of day, because that's exactly what will heal you. The strength of your convictions towards being blessed every day with beauty and grace from all areas of consciousness will help you immeasurably.

We want to say, too, the reasons for wanting to be healthy are because you have a wonderful world to enjoy while you're human, and this is not going to be any different when you get to the afterlife. In other words, <u>what you have is about the best place we have seen</u> when you factor in the joy in which you are capable of living.

Therefore, I will end with this phrase: <u>just be who you have become without the need to qualify it as any one thing or another</u>. Each individual has in them loads of personas that want to be heard. <u>Let them</u>!

We will help you find that joy any time you would like. Just ask for Dr. Jung. I make house calls!

Best wishes for a beautiful life,

Dr. Carl Jung

Thank you! May I ask follow-up questions?

Of course. We have a very specific way of getting your attention, through your very honest questions! That's another way we work with you in the world.

Do you represent an archetype to me and others? When you and other nonphysical authors say "we," do you mean the archetypes? Are you them?

The archetype of the Sage is involved in <u>all</u> of these sorts of transmissions. The Sage has many kinds of spiritual gifts, including the welcoming of information from nonphysical points of entry. The archetypes live in the "beyond" state, in a sense, treating themselves to bringing with them their powers of observation through the entry points into your thinking, behaving, and—above all—in your way of <u>feeling</u>. The archetypes are there <u>always</u>.

We come and go, us personas. We can best be described as "personas of selfhood," not specific archetypes, although the archetypes are involved.

Thank you. Would you like to say something about "ascension," which was mentioned by Hunter S. Thompson and Albert Einstein?

This is hugely important and why the others mentioned it. The description by Hunter S. Thompson[26] got to the focus of my work, which was defining the spiritual world as everything in the Universe, regardless of its location, up or down. The descending currents are as equally important as the ascending. Therefore, I would agree most heartily with his assumptions about the necessity as well as value of the many kinds of life around you in helping you every day.

Thank you.

This would hopefully mean you won't wait so long to continue our conversation!

I look forward to it, and will remain your servant,

Carl Jung

---

[26] Hunter says in Chapter 2: "The ascended masters are not the only ones who have something to give you. Each person in your path, each tree, has something to give you when you allow it to."

CHAPTER 11

Hildegard of Bingen:
Seeding the World with Monasteries

We'd heard from three scientists — Goethe, Einstein, and Jung — who along with Hunter S. Thompson had mentioned the concept of "ascension" or "ascended masters." Ascension is defined as the spiritual energy that transcends or moves physical beings "above" the material world into the spiritual world, or Divinity. But what is "descended" — material — is also Divine, as we are in sacred relationship with Nature and each other. Ascension energy is often characterized as masculine traits, and descension energy as feminine traits. Both are necessary for our personal and cultural health.

It seemed fitting to have some mystics weigh in. Hildegard came to mind as someone who fully embraced both kinds of energy. I'd written a musical about her with Paul that was performed by his sixth-grade class a few years before, so I thought she'd probably come through.

Hildegard of Bingen (1098-1179) was a German Benedictine abbess, visionary, writer, activist, and composer. She wrote theological and botanical texts that included the medicinal uses of plants, animals, trees, and stones. She wrote letters, poems, and liturgical songs for female choirs — and what might be the first opera — while supervising the transcription and illustration of her visions and teachings, sometimes called "visionary theology." In 2012, she was named a Doctor of the Church by the Catholic Church and canonized as Saint Hildegard.

I'd asked to speak with Hildegard and was surprised at who came through first: a collective energy called "The Order of the Rose." Rose had mentioned them in 2007 when I first began to channel her. She described them as a nonphysical collective of monastics whose intent is to inspire their continued legacy. The importance of nuns throughout the ages was a central theme of Rose's early on — how their roles have been diminished by the patriarchy in recent centuries, but how they were and will be a force to be reckoned with.

This had been an odd and concerning start to my channeling Rose, to be sure, as after twelve years of Catholic school, I was not *fond of nuns, some of whom were abusive. But I trusted Rose, and still understand, too, that she does not promote confinement or repression, but the liberation of women and men who are called to pursue a variety of monastic paths not currently available to them.*

The Order of the Rose: Try to see us nuns — us Hildegards, Roses, and others — as working for your benefit, behind walls sometimes[27], with very little spotlight on us. We are the ones who have kept things going for generations of you — all of you — in perfect harmony. The Mother of us all — the Blessed Mother of us all — the Divinity known as Ishtar, Eve, Asherah, all of them commit to the sanctity of our fellow creatures to potentiate the healthy unfolding of your world.

We have a wide variety of nuns in our order. Some are spun from pure magic — those who follow the advice of Nature, who summon spirits to bring

---

[27] Those who commit to monastic life sometimes live behind cloistered walls. During Hildegard's time, anchorites (usually women) committed to being permanently enclosed in their cells.

healing. The many kinds of nun include the beneficiaries of healing powers—the powers that you behold each day—the many kinds of spiritual counselors and artists of words and music. Every form of nun you can imagine has brought to your world some kind of artistry that is commendable as well as necessary.

We nuns, all of us, have this to say: <u>there will be more of us in the world, male as well as female, doing the work needed to move you into greater areas of peace, love, and full human potentials</u>. We speak for all the nuns here in order to ensure you have the best understanding of the power of nuns in your world.

We will turn our thoughts towards one who was there in history, one of the millions of sisters of faith who seek to mend the ways of the world—Hildegard von Bingen—who starts with a sobering message, perhaps, yet needed to help you move into the areas of expression you need to be in.

The path is needed this time around to help you move into the kinds of faiths you need to have: faith in love, faith in others, faith in Nature. We want to express, too, that the necessary "permissions"[28] are now in place for you to do more spiritually wonderful miracles that you so desperately crave. And now we will turn you over to Hildegard.

(The next section is from Hildegard.)

---

[28] Albert Einstein speaks about the concept of permissions in Chapter 9. There are similar references to "credentials" by Hunter S. Thompson (Chapter 2) and "protocols" by Ayn Rand (Chapter 3).

I love <u>all</u> of you for tending to your gardens in the way you have for so long without the necessary tools for implementing the harvests you need going forth in the world. My gardens — glorious ones, some vast in size — were part of our ministries that occupied beautiful monasteries back in Germany before you ever knew what Germany was. For my work was in the Rhineland, the beautiful valley between rivers[29] that spoke hundreds of years ago when cascading through the lives of the people who lived there, and spoke, too, throughout the world, as my work was disseminated throughout all parts of it.

My name is Hildegard of Bingen, the abbess and scholar who set forth the unruly notion that women should be protected under the law, and that we had valuable work to do in our homes and monasteries, too.

The work of women was something that I still profess, to this day, requires more honor. For what better model for forgiveness and humility — as well as service — is there but the woman who is sweeping your floors every day? What better person to aspire to than one who significantly stokes the health of all who live near her? The path for many is in service to others, yet there's no greater privilege or honor than being a "common" — and I use that word in quotes —

---

[29] Hildegard was tithed (donated) to the Catholic church when she was about eight years old. She was fifteen when she joined the Benedictine monastery, Disibodenberg, located between the Nahe and the Glan rivers. She and several nuns left Disibodenberg to found their own, nun-run monasteries: Rupertsberg (located between the Nahe and the Rhine rivers) in 1150 and Eibingen (in the Rhine Gorge) in 1165.

housewife, for <u>she supports the world in ways no other human ever did</u>.

So, with that, let me move into another topic which has held sway in my world, too: the plight of women in particular.

The reality of your patriarchy, as some have mentioned already[30], has been to put people into win-lose situations, when the reality is you don't need to go there at all. The zero-sum game, as it is called now, has perfectly placed each person who does <u>not</u> play the game into untenable situations that require meaningful change. The changes have to do with looking out after those you consider small or unimportant.

What would your world look like if there'd be no paying attention to the small things? What would your world be like if you were only to pay attention to your own sense of achievement, of being better at something, perhaps a novel you're writing or a challenge you've given yourself? What indeed would the world be like?

Each time you take up the matter of small things, the large things will take care of themselves.

I knew what to do about small things and large things, too. My monasteries were the biggest buildings in all of the country, and yet each time I sought to repair, say, a sapling that had fallen over, or righted a wound that someone was suffering from, I took care of the small things, too. This is what you all need to do to be happy.

---

[30] Ayn Rand provides references to patriarchy in Chapter 3.

146

The persistent, achievement-oriented goals are not going to help you if in their course they do not include, for example, taking care of your everyday tasks: getting food, cleaning your home, all of the things that are important to do. Yet what do you do? You say, "This is beneath me, this cleaning of my home. This is beneath me, this taking care of my family members. This is beneath me, this folly of not only living for myself but living for others, too." This is the result of cultural values that are overly focused on the ascending masculine currents of Divinity, and this has grown into a colossal problem in your world today.

The basics are these: <u>the best path needs you to be on it without caring overly much about the goals you seek</u>.

The reasons are these. You need to be in the world. To escape through thinking that you first need to be a perfect individual, even, will not help you at all. The imperfections of yourself and the world are crying out for you to embrace them and to bring them into the light of healing and responsibility that encourages their own growth and happiness.

This was something I did when I was physical, and I was the best example I can think of, as a monastic abbess who built monasteries, staffed them, and sought to commune with the spiritual dimensions every chance I got. I understood the need for strength and sensitivity. I understood the need to stand up to the bullies in my day and to strike out against those who sought to oppress others. I struck out when needed — in the most masculine way possible — while still remaining a sensitive and thoughtful woman who was there to serve. The acclimation of both the "eros" and "agape," therefore, was imbedded in my very core of being.[31]

The way to view this nowadays in your world is as the need to have both strength and sensitivity, as I said. And this will result in a more just world, too, because you can't ignore the vulnerable who are at risk and continue to put your own satisfaction first if you only focus on the latter. You need to step out of this selfish way of being in the world, some of you, and learn to be a force of Nature.

This had everything to do with how I ventured into monastic life. The monasteries of my day were the kinds of places you need today, for they were beacons of light in a very dark world, and you need these again. I had gardens—mainly gardens of food, medicine, and people who grew into the most beautiful kinds of practitioners. Still more gardens resulted in the beneficiaries of our kindness who sought to be self-supporting, and we taught them that, too. The purpose of my saying all this is, the monasteries and the gardens were needed then, and they are needed now.

This is what I did when I was alive. I helped each person who came through our doors, whether or not they deserved it, in a sense. They were cheats and robbers, some of them, yes, but they provided us the ability to do God's work. And in my studies, I helped myself as well to the ingrates in spirit—those who

---

[31] The Greek word *eros* is described by Plato as an appreciation of the beauty within a person that inspires one towards a spiritual plane of existence and is associated with ascending masculine energies. *Agape* is a Greek word for love connoting brotherly love or charity and is associated with descending feminine energies.

persecuted me through my thoughts of devils, when the reality was, the devils were never the kinds of serious threats that those who were living at the time were — the popes, the kings, the emperors — those who oppressed others through their wealth.

This still happens, and you need to throw it off, too. In the words of Thomas Paine, "All people deserve liberty." All people deserve a living wage, too. And in this, our monasteries also provided people a place to recover as well as to provide their service to the world.

These monasteries were not like those you have today. They were healing places, primarily, stocked with foods such as homemade jellies, and other garden products such as fresh, healing herbs and teas. Bacon and other worldly goods were sometimes delivered by the local farmers in reciprocation for the work we did. There were biscuits baking all the time, and many kinds of breads, too.

Honestly, there was every reason to believe those monasteries were heaven on earth, and that's what I sought to provide, and I did provide, and I still provide this in ways that you might find funny: <u>I will them into being</u>.

This is not the same way as I did when physical. I set the priority that there will be more monasteries like this, and I will them through my thoughts and deeds each day, in this heavenly space I've created here, much like the life I lived on earth, too. I will these things by continuing to focus on the visions I had when physical, the visions of light and of separation from the evils of the world. I set forth on my journey with vigor and I never stopped, even for a moment. I still take on the kings, and popes, and bishops, and all of them who seek to suppress us nuns.

And this was what I learned: that there's nothing that I couldn't do! <u>There's nothing that you can't do, either, and to expect something to occur has power to it!</u>

This is why I say, "I will these things into being." It's through my very spirit that some things came to be — before, as well as after, my physical life — and this may sound unusual in any situation other than in this book which you are reading. However, you have a grasp by now that past, present, future, all are tied together in purposeful, beautiful ways, and I have the kind of power that I can use for the betterment of people in each timeframe I will myself into. This means, of course, I'm willing myself into yours now with the intention of seeding the world with monasteries like mine that serve others.

The path for me included, as well, the embrace of the visions I had, then I had them committed to artistic works to be viewed and appreciated. My work included the kinds of scholarly works that I'm known for, channeling, as it were, the spheres of influence our writer is doing here as well. I sought to exchange my suffering for the works that came through me.[32] However, the suffering was not needed: only my full immersion was. So please don't think this is necessary for you: it is not. Try to consider your gifts as those which come freely, unselfishly, and joyously without suffering. The path for you, therefore, has many roads that intersect with your own, and your path will show you which to take.

---

[32] Hildegard's visions have been described as her ability to view the ordinary world and the visionary world at once, with eyes wide open in waking state. But doing so, she suffered from what may have been severe migraines.

I will also say, though, that the future has more monasteries in it. The path for you may not go there. However, you will be the beneficiaries of these centers of community, these Temples of Love that heal as well as nurture those around you. And if by chance you see some beautiful works of art, then celebrate them, too! Music, for me, was the most important thing, because the ringing of the sounds of our chorus met the walls of those places in ways that were truly transcendent. There's no greater art than the singing of people!

Without needing to tell you more about what to do about the world now, I will simply say this: the expectation that you can make these centers happen will be the way to go forward. <u>Try to see each community as needing a center for you all, then enjoy making this come into being</u>. I will help, of course, from here, in my own beautiful space, watching over you.

May God protect you and heal you.

With loving thoughts,

Hildegard von Bingen

CHAPTER 12

Paramahansa Yogananda:
The Guru in You

Paramahansa Yogananda (1893-1952) was an Indian yogi who introduced millions of people in the West to the teachings of his spiritual lineage. He was sent by his lineage masters to demonstrate the unity between Eastern and Western religions and to preach a balance between Eastern spirituality and Western materialistic achievement. He founded the Self-Realization Fellowship (SRF) / Yogoda Satsanga Society (YSS) of India and lived his last 32 years in the United States. Coincidentally, the Waldorf school in which my husband, Paul, taught for ten years sits on SRF property in Pacific Palisades, California, and the nearby Lake Shrine is a treasured place for us to visit.

I'd recently read Autobiography of a Yogi *by Yogananda, which I loved, so you'd think it would be obvious to me that he'd come through. But I had trepidation because I didn't know if I'd be able to live up to his expectations as a mystic... I do not have the discipline of his acolytes! What happened next was unique compared to the other authors. It was as if he was teaching me how to go into a deepened state, even though I wasn't immediately sure who was coming through.*

We suggest you take a few deep breaths to prepare: no requirement other than that is ever necessary. There's no need to read any books. Just allow yourself to feel into the personal space the energy occupies.

Okay.

Do you know who we are now?

Yogananda.

The way you have of determining this is what?

I feel you. I've gotten to know you in the book, and I sense your personality and how you "sound."

And do you give me credit for some of your thoughts?

Some that I associate with what I've read, but others, no. Why do you ask?

I was not wanting you to feel lacking, only to suggest that more of your everyday thoughts come from others besides you.

I'm getting used to that idea. We're taught to fear thoughts we attribute to not being "our own." I suspect my grandmother was, like me, sensitive to psychic energies, but like most people had little or no understanding of her gifts and was troubled and withdrawn from the world.

This is why we mention it. The path for her was not an easy one. Her karma was to engage with the world in ways that helped intensify the battles that many individuals engage when they choose lifetimes that are tremendously gifted, and she was that: tremendously gifted.

Her ability to connect with spiritual energies overrode her ability to connect with humans, and this was torturous for her. The attitudes of early nineteen-hundreds in the United States were on the most part not even open to who she was.

The facts remain, too, that many individuals who suffer in hospitals have the same gifts, they just haven't received the guidance they need to bring about the kinds of changes required to allow this human potential to emerge in the world. Take heed to share what you can — with your own abilities intact — to help others. This has been a big lesson in your life.

Yes. I also have to continually be discerning about what comes through, and I'm not quick to believe it is who it says it is. Also, when the ideas are similar to things I've wondered about, I wonder if it's me who's thinking these things, not the person coming through.

This is due to the fact that you're allowing a lot of voices in your mind all the time, and you listen as I did when I was alive on earth, and still do, because I understand things in the same way. I don't potentiate the thoughts. I <u>hear</u> them only: <u>they are from God</u>. If you want to think about this differently, hear these words as the words of God, only spoken in the languages of one another, not from "on high" as much as translated for our benefit and that of others.

Thank you. And this has to do with the fact that we're all One. Jung might relate this to what he calls the collective unconscious.

Yes, the Jungian information was available in my time, too. In the discussions from his chapter, I have surmised our audience might want to hear a bit more about the sorts of eminent characters inside their own personalities, those with which I have lived with for many years.[33]

I was not the sort of yogi that many have become these days. I had another kind of training that was deepened by the practice of Kriya Yoga[34] and that is what helped me to reach the areas of perception that I dwell in still. Do you have a sense I'm speaking with you now, in my own voice?

Absolutely.

Then imagine for a moment how you would feel in my presence in the material sense, to help you gaze at your yogi with the deepest of affection.

(This moved me to tears.) This affects me profoundly, my guruji.[35]

The reason we have for doing this very exercise in the transmission of the texts of the Yogoda Satsanga[36]

---

[33] Yogananda speaks of his interactions with his teachers and others who were no longer physical in *Autobiography of a Yogi*.

[34] Kriya Yoga includes many techniques to rapidly accelerate spiritual development. These include meditation, yoga postures, breathing and concentration techniques, and social and moral practices.

[35] My words surprised me, as I've never considered myself an acolyte of <u>anyone</u>. I've seen so many abuses. However, in this state of communion with Yogananda, to call him my guruji was perfectly fitting and sincere.

[36] "The teachings of Yogoda Satsanga Society of India (Self-Realization Fellowship) are founded upon the original Yoga of Bhagavan Krishna and the original Christianity of Jesus Christ.

lineage is to silence those who wish to demote them to the lowest forms of spiritual awareness, when in reality, our very souls have purpose in extending to your current experiences the same potentials for spiritual advancement.

There's no need to do more than you can with what you already have. Some individuals understand the process of connecting with greater Selfhood and claim it as their own. However, we will make sure you understand before this chapter is through that you have so many more avenues available to you to potentiate the happiest and most fulfilled selves you can imagine.

Will you follow the lineage of the yogis who came before you? Yes, if you care to adapt your lives to the personhood you have claimed as your God, yet you do not really know or feel directly connected to. The proper way to do so is to do exactly what this girl is doing and to see your Gods as the loving yogis they are, because this is a more accurate translation of the God-person relationship. <u>The realization that Godhood is loving is the first step in realizing oneself</u>.

The interpretations of your Scriptures have left much to be desired. For example, the properties of your planet now, the very elements that make your world what it is, the atoms that you think are so very stuck into your forms are not at all that. They are like a gossamer veil that sweeps into view the very thoughts you think and the very things you dream of.

The spiritual lineage of YSS/SRF consists of these two great avatars and a line of exalted masters of contemporary times: Mahavatar Babaji, Lahiri Mahasayaji, Swami Sri Yukteswarji, and Paramahansa Yoganandaji (last in the line of YSS/SRF Gurus)." - *yssofindia.org*

The properties, therefore, of your material world are continually transient and are there to help you see through the clouds of mystery into the deeper truths of who you are. The connections, therefore, between atoms are formed by love for all things: the Love of the Universe.

Take for example the gurujis who I was devoted to. They were able to transmute the bodies of their physical lives, to shed them without any suffering, to move beyond this material world into the subtle realms so as to let go of the physical world instantaneously. Suffering was not needed, nor is it ever.

The suffering you do to writhe out of your bodies, in a sense, is unnecessary. The reason we say this is you see too much "suffering out of the body" these days on your television sets. This is not necessary. The physical world is impermanent — illusionary. "Maya"[37] is what we call it, and while being this, it is also the most material world you can imagine.

What is it about this physical world that makes it both real and nonreal? We will help you get the full impact of the situation you're in so you can treat yourselves to the very depths of spiritual advancement in this short chapter.

The treadmills of your world are there for your experience. The situation of suffering is not to hurt or to execute a deep penance. The suffering is for you to stop wherever you can.

---

[37] "*Maya* is sometimes referred to as 'cosmic delusion' ...the power in creation by which limitations and divisions seem to exist in the Oneness that is true reality." – Paramahansa Yogananda, *Autobiography of a Yogi*

The world is therefore a kind of "allowance for learning" that it is not required in the sense of penance, but a choice you make as spiritual beings. The promise is to rise through the suffering into nonsuffering, and this is achieved through yoga as well as other gentle exercises in consciousness raising. The provocation of suffering that you endure will end eventually. However, you won't find any better way to provoke instead your own depths of being as well as fulfillment.

Therefore, the potential for suffering can be erased by the very act of yoga and can be reasonably managed, too, by ensuring your glorious beings have the kinds of commerce that allow you to help the world in the best ways you know how. We did this through our teachings — all of us in the lineage — and we helped to educate the West in our travels into the United States.

The provocation of lineage was a very heady topic. Lineage is not exactly what you might think. This here — this teaching you're reading now — is a lineage. However, getting the teachings from a master in person is what we would call ideal.

Your educational system, therefore, could be expanded to include the teachings of yoga by lineage holders without too much fuss, and we would love to see this transpire. However, the cost may not be practical, so why not enjoy a few lessons from your new guruji?

First of all, take time in the morning and evening to meditate. This is the only rule of yoga, really, in that this will help you team with spirit to induce a kind of love for yourself and all things. Twice a day will do.

Next, adopt an internal code that ensures you have the connection throughout the day. "Dreaming in daylight" will be what we term to be this feeling tone. The stacks of memories you have continually dwelled on do not need to be: find a way to get around your continual thinking in circles. This will benefit you immensely.

Next, try to eat safe foods, meaning the kinds of food that feed your body well without too much of the sugars and other fillers that only help to pollute the planet. There are sacred foods. Find them.

Lastly, dream until your dreams come true. There is a saying in Sanskrit: "Those who dream have enough to wake them from death." The way we see this is as "turning to your immortal Selves will help you move from suffering to grace."

The reasons for coming through this channeler here has to do with our work as another kind of teacher, an author who was not exactly the kind of person you would think would connect so deeply with the West. However, we were exactly the kind of person who would connect deeply with the West.

The reason we say this is: you have those kinds of things ahead of you, too. You don't think you're the person who would be successful at this, but you will be. Trust that we here—all of us yogis, all of us helpers—will do exactly what's needed to help you at all times. We did this while on earth, and we do this still. However, you need to reach out to us. That's all you need to do, and we will be here when you need us.

Now, the experts in religious comparative literature understand the nature of Christianity and how it compares to the religions of the East. In simple terms, they are the same. However, Christian dogma has superseded all understanding of the deeper truths of the Christ figure, and this has caused great suffering.[38]

The Christ you know was the same kind of yogi we were, and the same yogi who was expert at restoring sight, for example. He was a healer who committed to the Eastern ways of the yogi and had many episodes of sheer transcendence. He was able to move beyond where most yogis go, which made him special among them. The articles he left behind him — the stories, the many reports of his miracles — are very accurate. The specialness of his character was something to behold!

Now, we have a similar Christ figure in our lineage and that is Babaji, the wholly present transfiguration of the ancient teacher who has found both physical and nonphysical life in the world. He has transmuted into another kind of yogi who can be in more than one place at a time, can lift the veils of maya, and can easily find persons who need him.

You have the ability to call on this form of Christ if you want to, this wholeness of personhood to help you every day. For example, the traditions of your Christianity have helped you to connect with the Source of Love in the form of your Jesus Christ. This is the same character, in some ways.

The truth of Christ, therefore, isn't a person, it's a state of being, a wholeness of being that transmits to you the very awareness that you're seeking. <u>The Christ, therefore, is in you, not somewhere else</u>.

---

[38] Yogananda wrote much about Jesus Christ, including the books *The Second Coming of Christ* and *The Yoga of Jesus: Understanding the Hidden Teachings of the Gospels.*

Do you see the difference, and how important the distinction is? You don't have to suffer to get to where Jesus is now. You are where Jesus is now when you abide by his own teachings and live like Yeshua[39] did then, as a simple person who had nothing but goodness to share. You can do this, too. You only need to follow the ways of the yogis like he did.

Jesus, therefore, understood the ways of Hindu religion before they were Hindu, the avataristic[40] principles that were in full bloom during his day. The shedding of his corporeal body was also something he did. However, he did not need to be crucified to fulfill the prophecy. He only needed to shed his body in the same way that advanced yogis have done for thousands of years. The patterns of his life follow this tradition. I will share a bit more about his life.

He was dedicated to the temple at the age of twelve. This has been noted as a visit to the temple of Jerusalem, however this was only a brief stop before going further into the Eastern country of what is now India. Reduced to a mere acolyte, he was studied in the works of his own tradition and therefore was able to comparatively study both in his own tongue and works, as well as that of the sacred teachings of ancient India. The purpose for this was similar to the purpose

---

[39] The name Yeshua was popular among men of Jesus's time. It corresponds to the Greek *Iesous*, from which, through the Latin *Iesus*, becomes the English *Jesus*.

[40] The Sanskrit word "avatar" means "descent." According to Yogananda, it signifies the descent of Divinity into flesh, and that an avatar "is born not to show us how great he was, but to give us hope that the state of consciousness he had attained, we too can attain." – Paramahansa Yogananda, *Autobiography of a Yogi*

to my life: <u>to take the teachings back to where the people needed them the most</u>.

The Semite people had always been affiliated with Indian ways, and indeed this was due to the very nature of the migration from India to where they are now. In other words, the Semite and Indian people were cousins of sorts, and the ways were very similar, when you really get down to it.

The Semites of that time were the same as us, only did not have, at some point, the inquisitiveness that comes from the teaching that supposes the immaterial world had better lives ready for them. The persecutions of many other peoples were among the ways in which this was expressed.

However, the Christ figure was there to help correct the problem and did so in some ways. The forces around the Christ figure suggested another kind of revolution, and the movement was to some degree quelled by the acts of violence that were brought to bear on the followers.

Now, this era that you live in now is karmically forged with the times of your Jesus Christ. The lectures he gave were focused on the achievement of human compassion and the transcendent world that would accommodate all who wished to go to where — he said — the Father was.

The same Father is still the focus of my lineage, the Father of us all. And the Father still remains the best of what we have to provide, while at the same time we also honor the Divine Mother. The patriarchal systems, therefore, are beginning to turn more towards the Divine Mother aspect of us all that is the expression of descending currents of energy, rather than the focus on the ascension that we have spoken about in terms of Jesus and other yogis.

The facts are that the issues are similar now, something that the world has to get past, and there's not any reason to believe anything that you hear except that which you have asked your inner world — your inner gurus — to help you sort through. In other words, <u>you are learning to assimilate the teachings of the ancients with the truths or nontruths you hear every day</u>. You're learning again how to live like a yogi. You're allowing yourselves to be free of fear and suffering. You're gaining wide swaths of understanding of the world as maya. You're breathing the air around you differently, more as an intake of Godhood.

What else do you want in a guru? In fact, the guru in you is wanting very much to speak to you: <u>let them</u>! When you're ready, simply imagine us or another guru — such as Jesus — to provoke in you a sense of deep love and connection. You can imagine them as they are or will be when you see them in the world beyond this one. You don't have to die, though: you only need to connect with them deeply <u>now</u>.

We want to say, too, the paths for many include the opportunity for monastic life and we suggest this is helpful. When you can, try to learn more about what it takes to live simply, to gather simply, to eat simply, and to breathe in the love of all things every day. This mood has many physical benefits, too, because you will let go of much of your stress every day. What better thing to accomplish than that?

We will say, too, the spiritual life is not what you have thought it was, perhaps. The spiritual life is the life you live every day, only without the suffering. Allow it to help you.

Thank you, guruji! Three questions for you. First, can you comment on the male-centric nature of your lineage? In your life, you honored women, and some followed similar monastic paths. But the legacy of denial of certain paths to women continues to be a big problem. Can you address this? Second, you mention Einstein in your own book, and I wonder if you'd like to comment on the similarities of your views. Third, you mentioned in this passage "dream until your dreams come true" which is a lyric from a popular song by Aerosmith. Were you aware of this when you said it?

We will give you the answers in the reverse order that you asked them. Yes, we have access to the inspired thoughts from many of the collective who have been helping with these transmissions. The Aerosmith band is known to me. Therefore, this was chosen as a means to help you understand fully the real integration of the yogic path into your own culture. This should not be taken for granted in spite of the form it takes, which for us is wonderful, as you know and love the people in this group that has played this song for you so lovingly. Enjoy knowing these were inspired actions, too.

Next, the Einstein of your times was the same as mine only a bit more advanced in age. This did not matter because the thoughts themselves were of cosmic order and therefore were timeless. Thus, whenever he "preached his lessons" (and we say this to be humorous, but it's true that he carried God with him, too) he was able to impugn the nature of materialism in ways that suggested wisdom in the sense of materialism itself. This was the result of science and did not imply yogis sitting around waiting for God to come calling. No, <u>this was rationally conceived—so they thought</u>—and that was the language required to spread the word of the immaculate Cosmic action of reciprocity, which was communicated through the theory of relativity.

<u>Next, yes, women have a very huge role to play in the coming years in your world!</u> The actresses who have taken a stand[41] are displaying yogic kinds of thinking, even. Role models for women are now emerging fully in the form of disciples of goodness rather than as exploited beings of materialistic patriarchy.

Always consider that the Divine Mother is another form of the great Buddha, Krishna, and all the forms of love of all things, too. She will be your guide whenever you need her as well.

Thank you!

You're very welcome. We will visit whenever you would like for us to.

With kindest regards,

Paramahansa Yogananda

---

[41] The Me Too social movement against sexual abuse and harassment began in 2006 and had made major headlines. It was supported early on by a number of high-profile actresses. The movement inspired change in many areas of business and culture around the world.

CHAPTER 13

J. D. Salinger:
You Have Magic in You

Yogananda's thoughts reminded me of J.D. Salinger's, with whom I wrote The Afterlife of J.D. Salinger *in 2016. I sensed he'd want to write a chapter, and I looked forward to it. It was because of Salinger that I learned to communicate in depth with nonphysical persons like him. The learning process was intimate, careful, and respectful, as we were, after all, strangers to one another.*

Jerome David Salinger (1919-2010) has always had a lot to say. He was an American author of articles, short stories, and novels, including his most influential, The Catcher in the Rye. *His work was informed by his service as a U.S. soldier in some of the most terrible conflicts of World War II. As I described in our book, he "guided post-world war young people, especially, to think independently and meaningfully, to reject inauthenticity, to love deeply, to consider that even the simplest acts of kindness carry in them great divinity."*

At the end of his life, Salinger lived in seclusion, spending much of his time writing in a kind of bunker on his New Hampshire property. In The Afterlife of J.D. Salinger, *he talks about his afterlife environment, the process he went through to get there, and how he is still writing in the same kind of bunker he had when physical.*

I had the most delightful time dictating *The Afterlife of J.D. Salinger*, as well as in creating the kind of conversations that you and I were able to continue.

Would you like to say more about this? Because this has to do with what I'm going to talk about today.

Yes, thank you! You and I have had several spontaneous "inner" conversations since writing our book. I have the weird ability to hold conversations in my head with people who are nonphysical. I'm able to concentrate on both sides of a conversation between me and someone else.

Yes, and you have this ability to do so with everyone else, don't you?

Yes, so far.

So, you have multiple personalities in you, would you say?

Yes, in me, or through me.

This is something that you might want to share with our readers. The portal between you and the nonphysical is very wide, and you need to sometimes express the ways in which we come through as <u>always</u> being allowed, not ever intrusive, right?

Yes, it's always at my request. When I began to channel, and encountered unhelpful energies, I literally told them to "fuck off." Now I'm less fearful, and kinder. I say, "Thank you but you're not being helpful. Please go where you will be healed."

That's a helpful way to set up what I'm going to be talking about, which is why I asked you the questions. In your view, do you have any reason to ignore the many voices, even the nonhelpful ones?

Not really, because they've been helpful in their own ways. They remind me to go into a higher state of Selfhood. I'm thinking of something you said in our book about the value of "nonhelpful" voices. It's my favorite part.

Sometimes religious thinking has you tied up in the belief that there's a rodent in each of us that needs killing. This is preposterous because rodents, even, have their place in the world. So you try to kill the rodent in you, when the reality is that you need to be friends with the beautiful creature who is so sadly misunderstood. You need to engage it to say, 'I know you have reasons for being here. I want to help you be who you need to be, too. You can't just go around infesting my life with your little nests, though. So I will take you lovingly into a space where you can thrive and have nests of joy in your beautiful space.'

That's all there is to it. The beasts in us all have reason to live.

That's so beautiful.

Do you realize that these are aspects of <u>yourself</u>? That even the sad, lonely aspects that you speak to sometimes are part of your overall Selfhood?

Yes, but it gets tricky to call them all "Self" when someone like you — with a name and death date — comes through. We humans seem to require the distinctions to think about it. We barely have the language for it.

This is why you have the people coming through you now: to help you provide some clarity around the phenomenon that we are participating in.

You're all of us. We're you, too. We have another kind of aspect self to us in that we have more of the access to higher thoughts than you do right now, because that's the state we're in. However, <u>you have the ability to access this, too</u>. You do this through your own self, your own Joanne, all the time, whether or not you call it that. And we want to suggest that you have the ability to tell our readers more about this phenomenon because <u>they have this ability, too</u>. That's what this is all about.

And if you do this, maybe you can have some clarity around your whole life more than you do. What more might you do than help to wake up the people who need to contact the Self they know loves as well as protects them always? What better way to grow into a new phase for yourself, to contact the dead in ways that are wantonly beautiful in their expressions of love for humanity?

No one has the full truth of any situation. There are only wider or narrower versions — or "aspects" — of the same thing. That's what the Selfhood we talk about consists of.

The sense of discernment you have has been developed over time, with experience. Most people who have the same abilities don't fully understand that they need to be discerning, to continually determine whether or not an aspect is being helpful or merely acting out, in a sense. This is something that needs to be learned, just as you learn about other aspects of yourself, such as the child in you who sometimes needs more loving, gentle discipline. These are all necessary topics to consider when doing this kind of work.

Yes, and some people end up in mental hospitals.

Yes, they don't understand the acuity needed to sort out what is coming through, when the reality is, it's typically one's higher Self, just in different forms or aspects so as to ensure the person has the best experiences they can.

The model of the psyche you're relating is consonant with Carl Jung's and has the potential to help a lot of people.

All of your aspects can be helpful: you just need to know how to engage them.

Yes, that's it.

The full expression of aspects in the physical framework has ways of getting your attention.

Thank you, Mr. Salinger.

You may call me Jerry.

Thank you, but I can't! It's too weird! Maybe someday.

Well then, let me just say you're fine doing whatever you're doing, as long as you want to.

With that, I will continue with the topic of Selfhood and how this played out in my lifetime. I have gained so much since the so-called death of my physical body, which was not exactly dead, let's say, but filled with the essence of Self, as I was while alive. The physical body gave way to the essence of who I was, which included my physical identity, which I took with me. You might call my present self a ghost of who I was then, only lighter, with less suffering.

I had experienced another kind of world when I was alive. I had the same kinds of thoughts about nonexistent people, those who lived only in my imagination. They were the Glass family, and they were as real to me as anybody I knew who was physical. The same way that my hero in *The Catcher in the Rye*, Holden Caulfield, felt to me, he felt to you, too. And he was somebody who had a great deal of influence on many millions of people. Who can say he's not real?

I have brought myself into this realm of being, this situation in which I am speaking to you now, in order to find a way to help all of you understand the importance of knowing that <u>you're not alone, ever</u>. The way I lived was solitary, thinking that I could engage my deepest Selfhood, and I did. However, I did not realize that I needed to also be in the world, as everyone around me served as another aspect. If I had been able to fully see that, I would have been another kind of person. I would have been more assured that I was loved. However, I was also embraced by the Glass family, and that was the most real experience for me, more than I felt in my own family.

The facts about the afterlife are these. You will not die. The path you take will be whatever needs to occur to help you to heal and move onward into the kind of wonderful space I'm in now. If you have a need for another kind of life that you would not have had before, you can do that, too. The present moment ends up being the best one you can imagine.

See, that's what this whole thing is about: <u>allowing yourself to enjoy the moment</u>. The world here helps you to do that more than ever because you have only that, really, not the distractions of time and space in the way you know them now.

The changes you will go through exceed your imagination, they really do. The course of your planned exit — and I do mean <u>planned</u>, nothing escapes the planning of your passage, this is totally pre-thought out — into the afterlife is not so much about leaving the worst behind as it is the allowance for less troubled thinking. This is wonderful to us here, because we can get fully into the beauty of life without worrying too much. Oh, we still worry, and that's what I'd like to talk about now.

The reasons for my saying "we worry" has to do with why we come through this channeler here, this remarkable woman who extends herself so fully into the ether that she makes waves in the spaces we occupy. The riches she brings incorporate the kinds of loving intention that we want to see more of in the world. Therefore, we here — we "physically challenged," to make a joke — have reasons to want to encourage more of the kinds of acts of greatness that the person typing these words is doing, and to allow yourselves to do them, which is what we want to talk about next.

These kinds of world-changing actions will not start out with a lot of gusto. The changes the world requires now — in this time of great suffering — will be about the kinds of small, loving kindnesses that you each do on a daily basis. These acts of humility, these wonders of the civilized world, are the things that you can do to ensure that every day will be a blessing for you or somebody else. In each case, we want to help you, because that's why we continue to be with you: to help you, dear people of the earth.

The likeness between myself now and J.D. Salinger is great. However, there will need to be some changes in your thinking to fully interpret what we will say next: the likeness between you and your own demised self is the same as ours. You live here, too. You exist in a state of otherness, of timeless unity. So you are here with us as much—or more—as we have proven that we are here with you. Which brings me to my next point: this is about your own savior Self coming to rescue you.

I took a lot of notes from the Hindu teachings, the Vedas being the most important things I ever read. In them—as you will find if you read them—the prayers for the dead are not as much about seeing them through difficult times of passage, because there was no fear in these earlier peoples about death. The books mostly focus on the ability for the dead to transcend their suffering so they can help you on earth still. This is about motivating others to be better, to be healthier, to be more fully alive.

This has been the most treacherous time on earth, perhaps. This terrible feud between people has taken too many lives, and too much harm has come to those who fight against those who oppress others. This is not going to end anytime soon. However, it will get better soon.

The reason why it will get better soon is because you're allowing more of your greater, more

173

nonphysical aspects of yourselves to come through you so as to tend to your situations more easily and with less suffering. You have encouraged more Selfhood by the very things you think about when you see yourselves as good. You allow more intentional actions. With each breath you take, you gain more love for self and the world. Do you see how the very things you're thinking now contribute to the beauty of the world? If you don't, you really should!

Now, I find the most remarkable thing about your world—your physical world—is the realization that you have more to you than you ever thought possible. You don't see this the way I do. For example, you think you exist in your own skin only. That's the worst way to consider yourselves.

This is a bit more of a lecture than I want to give, but hear me out because I will startle you with something, and that is that you have magic in you, all of you! You can use this magic to assume the kinds of superhuman things that you see on your television sets. You have these abilities. Why not use them?

The reason this sounds a bit lecture-y is because you can't hear this enough. You have to get this through your heads: <u>you have the ability to literally move mountains</u>, you're just not always seeing this as possible.

Here's how to open yourselves up to this kind of thing—this amazing world—that awaits you. First, look to those who quietly practice the kinds of magical abilities that you know are real. Next, look to them for support in your own abilities. They want to help.

Next, try to move into these kinds of pursuits slowly, without a lot of fanfare. You will get seen eventually. For now, just start by putting a few new things out there, whether it's a new kind of thinking or new way to paint or dance.

This expression is the most important thing — the expression — not what others will say about this new thing you're doing. Do you follow? You will not need "likes." You will not need to be popular. You will only need to trust your higher Self that your thinking is guided by miracles.

Now, the way I see this coming about is going to shock you, perhaps. You will see the changes without needing to fight about it. The changes will happen as soon as enough of you start playing around with the higher power energy to make your world a better place, without needing to go any farther than your own neighborhood. Try to see this as an excellent way to do your own thing every day without feeling like you're doing nothing. You will be moving mountains.

The situation that you have found yourselves in — this megachurch bullshit, presidential malfeasance, the inequity between people — has, to every degree, been taken over by greater forms of personhood in your physical reality and in nonphysical reality. You only need to finish it off for good.

Take bold steps that are directed towards love, and you will do so without needing violence. This is the best kind of protest you can do.

The stakes are high. However, you have angels on your side!

With loving thoughts,

J. D. Salinger

CHAPTER 14

George Harrison:
Meditate and Create

Mr. Salinger had come to mind when pondering Yogananda and the ancient Vedic spiritual traditions. George Harrison also came to mind, as he'd been a student of Yogananda and other Eastern spiritual teachers. He believed in the afterlife, saying, "The living thing that goes on, always has been, always will be. I am not really George, but I happen to be in this body."

George Harrison (1943-2001) was an English songwriter, musician, and producer who achieved international fame as the lead guitarist of the Beatles. After their breakup, he released All Things Must Pass *and other critically acclaimed albums, organized (with musician and mentor Ravi Shankar) the 1971 Concert for Bangladesh (a precursor to benefit concerts such as Live Aid), and co-founded a film company with members of Monty Python.*

I had more than my usual trepidations, but a synchronicity gave me confidence. Paul and I decided to watch a movie biography of George, Living in the Material World. *In it, George is seen wearing buttons on his lapels depicting Yogananda, and Babaji, who Yogananda mentions in his chapter. In case it would help, I chanted "Hare Krishna" for several days before I sat down to start.*

The way I see things now, away from the physical world, is that I hadn't really caught onto what others were saying about this kind of psychic ability [mediumship]. The reason I didn't really care for it while physical was that it really didn't tell me much more than I knew when I was doing things like tripping or meditating. As I was very physically present, perhaps, I didn't need to feel like the physical plane could be any more infused with spirit, without needing, for example, to talk to a dead auntie.

The way I went about living in this world you're in now and I'm not now was that I wasn't really needing anything except myself, in a sense. I had a very wide experience in alternative consciousness, as I said, and therefore felt like I was in many ways always being attended to. The reason I say this is because this is new to me, this kind of psychic connection, this kind of writing, which I think is very wonderful.

So I'll continue a bit without needing to talk much about my experiences while on the planet, since these have been covered in great depth, too much for my taste, if you ask me. However, I will shed some light, perhaps, on who I was then, and who I am now, which is a different kind of George than I was when I was physical.

I had a very unique life, full of great ups and great downs. Mostly things were up. The path I took was wonderful, full of wonderful friends, lovers, quite many of each, and I had wealth and fame, too. The classic hero worship was very big when I was alive, however. I didn't like it much.

Having said that, fame is not what you might think it is. It helps you as you begin to be an artist or what have you. However, it doesn't really help you when you get famous. I would warn everybody now to not worry too much about fame because it's really overrated. I was not pushing my way to the top, so this was something that I was spared. However, I would not have wanted the fame if I could have just had the life I had, which of course wasn't happening.

The beauty of the world is something that I treasured, especially with the kinds of homes I lived in. I loved the homes I lived in, all of them, even those that were not as fancy or what have you. The home is where the heart is, and I believe this is true. To that end, I've endured a lot of suffering even in my homes, so these are not necessarily needing to be perfect all the time, but they do provide wonderful spaces for living one's life.

I can't say enough about finding a home you can live in without caring too much about safety. This was something that was a terror in my life. I was constantly doubting the safety in my home, and this turned into a nightmare. One evening when I was sleeping, I was attacked by a terribly fucked up person who had it in his mind to kill me. This was the result of another kind of fear that I've had to work on here, which was a fear of others doing exactly that, that was conjured up as an experience to help me get past the fear.[42]

However, I wasn't about to do this while I was alive. I had to move many miles away to get refuge and, even then, was constantly at odds with our neighbors. This was something I would have done differently had I known that I was going to be okay without needing to worry so much.

---

[42] According to many afterlife reports, personalized experiences are provided to help individuals through the process of becoming nonphysical. Salinger describes his experiences in *The Afterlife of J.D. Salinger*.

Seeing this differently has helped me and was something that I was able to push past in my afterlife. I was able to heal through this experience when I was physical to some degree. However, most of my healing has been since I have been nonphysical. I learned that to be in the world means to be in the world without trying to escape from it, and this was how I was able to realize passage into the heavens, you might call it.

Here I'm doing what I did when physical. I'm eating, sleeping, having encounters with those of the opposite sex, and everything musical that I did when physical, I'm doing here too. Now there are brighter lights and more colors, maybe. However, this is very much like my tripping feeling sense, a sort of nonphysical world of love and precious thoughts that are mainly helping everybody around here. Precious thoughts of loving intention are always here, always precious, always fully wonderful.

I have everything I need without needing anything that's urgent. I have everything I need without feeling I'm being instructed to do anything differently, or to feel that others are suffering as a result of my grace-filled home. I have whatever I need without feeling like it's going to be taken away or anything like that, the kinds of thing you might feel when you're alive in the physical world.

The rewards of meditation are great, it still helps me every day. The kinds of breathing techniques I learned are ones I do now. I have many friends here and I live for love only. That's all I do every day — live for love — which takes the form of music, mostly, and sensual pleasures. The many ways I had of getting inspired are the same ways I have now of doing the same thing.

There's not that much difference, really, between my world and yours, especially if you meditate. This is something that I swear by still and always will. So if you don't meditate yet, you really ought to consider it. This will help you with everything your life, your music, or whatever art you do, and with everybody around you, too. So that's all I will say, because this is entirely up to you. However, I have to say what is on my mind and that is that more people should be meditating. You will create a better world if you have the ability.

So I will not tarry with that any more. The reason I say "tarry with that" is because life really doesn't require anything that you don't want to be doing. Without the impulse to create, though, you will be missing out on a lot. So <u>meditate</u> and <u>create</u>. Those are the only two words of advice will give you.

The pleasure trips I had were famous, so I won't bore you with those. I had a lot of supercharged realizations through what I called my spiritual religious path, which was neither and both at the same time. The works of Paramahansa Yogananda and the many masters I was able to learn from indirectly and directly will be found in the future, I predict, to be the most inviting and helpful paths towards happiness. These teachers have more to them than anything I've ever come across, and will be likely the best teachers for you, too.

I have many reasons for saying this. One, they are accessible to all. Two, they have enormous gifts of relating the most wonderful stories and teachings. Three, they take the learner into the kinds of places you need to be, which in my view are to be present in each moment as best as you possibly can.

This is the best path for many of you, as it was for me. I can see from here that in the future more of you will be impressing upon yourself the need to be fully engaged in a spiritual practice, and these will be the best teachers you could ever ask for.

I have a lot of wonderful memories from my world — my physical world — that I lived in. These memories have cast themselves into my present situation with the kind of loving intention I was telling you about earlier. The many people I loved are here with me now, even though they are still physical. So I've been able to accommodate a kind of thrilling ability to realize them now, in my home space that I have here. I have the ability to see my friends, my wife, my son, and everyone whenever I want. This doesn't mean they are anywhere near being nonphysical. It's more of an actual time tripping thing they do when they are fully realizing me in their thoughts.

You do this, too. You have the kinds of abilities to project yourselves into all kinds of spaces which haven't at all been fully made nonphysical. There are many kinds of self-projections, I'll call them, that have the wonderful ability to help people connect from anywhere. In fact, this is a good example. I'm not in any way familiar with this woman who is meeting me in this self-projection space, and now we're meeting and having a conversation about my life now.

What if you could do this too? What if you could have a space where you were able to connect with anybody you wanted to? It's entirely possible, and I'm here to tell you — go for it — because you will love this kind of playful spiritual path that for me was so much fun and still is.

I want to say one more thing and that is that you have some massive problems now which need solving, and it won't happen unless you find a way to work with others in the world, to serve the planet in the way you need to. I'm not saying to join a band and hold concerts, because that's not something most people can do. I'm saying <u>find people you can have fun with while helping others</u>. This is going to be so important in the coming years that I can't say this strongly enough. The purpose of life is to enjoy it, yes. However, there are many people in terrible situations that you need to help. Find a way to do that.

Thank you for this and the many beautiful things you've given us. May I ask a few questions?

Yes, I have more than enough time for your questions, so please feel free to do this kind of dialog with me.

Thank you! Much of your music feels like it pulls us towards the spiritual, towards Godhood, Selfhood. What's your relationship with God now?

I know what you mean, and I had many more thoughts of Godhood then than I do now. For me now, it's understood, a given, that He is here with me forever as well as in the past, present, and future. My perspective now embraces Godhood more than I was able to when physical.

When I was physical, I had to continually remind myself that God was ever-present. Now I don't need to. Now I've gone beyond that requirement to reach Godhood. I'm not God now, I'm saying that I'm God like you have come to understand yourselves as God. I'm not-God as well. That's something that's not fully understood by anyone I've encountered along the way, the idea that we are God and not-God.

What I do now know is that He's infused in all of Creation, without needing to say mantras or do much of anything. I love God now more than ever, through everything I've been through. I needed to remind myself to fully live in the moment, so I don't need to do that anymore, which I encourage you to do, though, before you get here.

I have a lot of people ask me for things while I'm here, like I'm God, which I'm not. So, you don't need to feel like praying to George is the same as doing works in the world that help others. That's how to best pray to whoever you choose to. That's how you get past the loneliness and suffering of maya, to do works that transcend the world's suffering. That's how you move towards Godhood, not through mantras. They only help you to realize there's God-ness everywhere.

Now that you're nonphysical, when I hear your music, or sing your songs, I feel like I'm singing them with you, and imagine many people feel that way. In those moments, are we more connected with you, or with God/Self, or both?

The music I left still lingers with me here, and in some ways, I do still sing the songs. So in some ways, you can feel like I'm there with you when you sing. This is fine with me — however, I can't get in everyone's shower all the time! I'm joking, of course, but there's truth to the understanding that you create your own connections with your own Source. My music may help, but you're not necessarily trying to reach me, you're trying to reach your Source. I'm there to help you, that's all.

The same with you [Joanne]. You're not trying to make people follow you on Twitter. You're trying to help them connect with their own Source without you needing to be a guru. I think that's exactly how I chose to be in the world: as a helper, not a guru.

The reason I mention this is I understand the reasons for you to be doing this work, because you want to help others. There's not any reason for me to speak with anybody else who, for example, may think differently. I wouldn't support that. I won't come through somebody with an agenda of just making money. That's not what I was about and it's not what I'm about now. You and I have the ability to connect this way because our clouds of potentials of what we'd love to consider connect first, then pull us together like pieces of a puzzle.

It's more than the kinds of hierarchies that we create in the material world. It goes far beyond the thinking that you were all raised with about God being the ultimate to achieve, when the reality is, He's everyone you know.

We here, in our own physically nonphysical space, are here to encourage everybody to do this, to escape from the world's problems by tuning into their greater Selves, their Goodness, which I have tried to communicate in songs. Go listen to them again because they will help you. We here will sing them with you if you want, or sing them solo, it doesn't matter. What matters is that you feel better about everything.

That's very helpful, thank you. You believed in reincarnation when you were physical.[43] Do you still? Are you aware of other lifetimes?

I did believe in reincarnation when physical, and do as nonphysical, and have only this to say: it's the most real thing you might ever consider thinking about. To suggest to yourself that you're on a sort of "journey of aspects" that are all working and playing together is wonderful and something I have enjoyed quite a bit while nonphysical.

I have very many aspects, some of which are physically focused people, some are not, some are Godlike, some are not in the sense of how we were raised to believe that God is higher, wider, etc. I have many lifetimes I have remembered here, more than I did when physical. So, yes, I have many. I have some there with you, on your planet now. They tend to be those who want to express deeply the many kinds of religion that exist, meaning everything from the most minute botanical drawings that somebody might do out of worship for the many plants in the world, to those who are expressing this intent through the kinds of scholarly works that I loved when physical.

The main intent for us all has to do with our connection to spirit. This can be expressed in phenomenal ways, as diverse as I've suggested here, as well as in mystical seances, the arts, music, etc. The themes of my life had the same kind of religious urge

---

[43] In 1968, George said, "You go on being reincarnated until you reach the actual Truth. Heaven and Hell are just a state of mind. We are all here to become Christ-like. The actual world is an illusion."

towards art, which is now being expressed daily by these other individuals who are living now and are part of me now.

What is your relationship with John Lennon like now that you're both no longer physical?

We have many good times together, he and I. When I say "times," these are still time-based, however not in the same sense as you know. We have played together many times, and have the deepest of connections because, you know, we were brothers in spiritual ways.

The way to consider this is, you go as you, and you have many people with you that you love. He's one of them. He's not the same person he was, no one here is. So, this is a bit difficult to describe. He's somebody who has been sleeping well more than he did when alive. I say this because he was somewhat agitated when living, and he's more at peace now. Without needing to say more, I'll say only that he's with God more than he was before. That's all.

I have just one more thing to say and that is I cherish each individual who wishes me well. I feel that now that I'm dead physically more than I did when alive. I cherish everybody who listens to my music, I cherish your warm thoughts about me, and I cherish even your mildest thoughts about me. I feel that, and I will send you my loving thoughts, too.

With very beautiful blessings to each of you,

George Harrison

CHAPTER 15

Douglas Adams:
A Self-Described Goddamned Atheist

When I began to channel Rose in 2007, I had a brief experience channeling Douglas Adams, or perhaps more accurately, a wider version of him. I'd just read his book, The Long Dark Tea-Time of the Soul *and loved it, and him, and said so. He replied, "We love you, too, but don't get overly rabbity about it because we* are *you. We expect that you will be more than underwhelmed when you meet us in person."*

Douglas Adams (1952-2001) was an English writer and author of many books including The Hitchhiker's Guide to the Galaxy *series. He was an advocate for environmental conservation, and described himself as a "radical atheist," once saying, "Isn't it enough to see that a garden is beautiful without having to believe that there are fairies at the bottom of it too?" He was fascinated by the nature of reality, as expressed in his famous maxim: "There is a theory which states that if ever anyone discovers exactly what the Universe is for and why it is here, it will instantly disappear and be replaced by something even more bizarre and inexplicable. There is another theory which states that this has already happened."*

Adams' friend Dr. Richard Dawkins dedicated his book The God Delusion *to Douglas, whom he jokingly called "possibly [my] only convert to atheism." I was of course happy to hear from him again.*

I was not the funniest person to be around when physical, probably because I was always laughing more at what was being said and done by someone funnier. That's how I approach my experiences with what you're doing here. I don't see myself as the one with the main things to say. I see you, Joanne, as that person, and I am just here to help you to do that. My name is Douglas Adams.

When I was young, I had the most agreeable way of seeing people. I was happy most of the time. I was eventually able to put into writing the very feeling tone I had as a child: something slightly awkward, something funny, beautiful, and sometimes astounding. I had to feel into what my experiences were as a child to get to the places I needed to be with my writing. And I was able to really be there. So when I say, "where I needed to be," this was an actual place, but the kind of place which one feels rather than sees. If you can imagine that, and if you have read any decent book worth your time, you will understand that the places you visit when reading are real in every way.

The same thing is occurring now with this marvelous transmission. I was able to find her years ago, and we had a brief dalliance. However, I was not physical, so this only works to some degree and does not at all mean that there were bodily fluids shared. In any case, I was coming through her early on in her ability, let's say, and I was able to make a few funny comments that she loved very much. She had already loved me through my books. I'm not being immodest here. She really loved what I was <u>saying</u>. I was able to reach between her and the childhood I had that gave me

188

the feeling tone I was able to use in my writing, even when I was writing through her.

Now, to be specific, having said all that: I was not completely sure this would work out, her being physical and me being nonphysical. This is about the most long-distance "romance" you might ever imagine. What I will say, though, is that our interaction was <u>very</u> real. However, she was not fully into believing that at the time.

However, with her newfound abilities, she is now more aware that these interactions are really, really real. I can't expect any more from her except the things she does well, which is to help me say a few things about what the conditions here are like, and what the situation is with me being able to share with you — through her — what we'll bring to the world, or to at least some readers who I address now.

Readers, this is <u>real</u>. This is so very real that you can't even begin to assimilate what is real and what isn't anymore. If this is real, then why not Santa Claus and Elvis still being alive? Well, these are real, too. It's just a nonphysical <u>thing</u> (for lack of a better word) that is <u>real</u>, and you can't know otherwise because you can't prove it isn't.

Just a bit more about that, because this gets into a very big discussion that I would often have with my friend Dr. Dawkins, who was my very best friend in the world in the sense of having deeply ingested his form of scientific spiritualism, you might say, because he was deeply spiritual, as am I, the fact that we were self-described atheists notwithstanding.

Here's why. The fact that you have a body, brain, and commensurate abilities to determine the course of your life has the same reality as the fact that I have no physical body, some brain, and commensurate abilities to determine the course of mine. Whether or not I'm physical is beside the point: <u>I'm human</u>. See? I'm human because I <u>was</u> human and the part of me that <u>is</u> human is <u>still</u> human, there's no escaping that.

So what does this have to do with what you think of in terms of the afterlife, or even your own lives? Well, <u>everything</u>! The fact that you can see with your eyes has little to do with the brain.[44] It has to do with the perceptions you have towards the thing you're witnessing. This is nothing new in your academic areas. The principles of the observer effect and the probable cat that quantum scientists have been arguing about for decades will help you understand how this can happen.[45]

---

[44] Physicist David Bohm proposed that the physical universe exists fundamentally as an inner, subtle state of unlimited probabilities from which physical phenomena unfold according to the subjective actions of the observer. Bohm proposed that there are two sides to the brain that reflect this: the subtle side and the manifest material side. The subtle side is the quantum level or Universal Mind that produces the physical material world, including the brain. Like a hologram, each of us has the Universe enfolded in us and projects it as our physical environment. <u>Since our experience doesn't depend solely on physical reality, and what we see doesn't depend solely on our physical brain, we take our "hologram" with us when we become nonphysical</u>. This corresponds with many esoteric teachings, including those of Krishnamurti (a collaborator of Bohm's), Seth, and Rose.

[45] The *observer effect* is a term used in physics to describe the disturbance of an observed system by the act of observation, such as a measurement or human observation. For example, some physicists suggest that the beliefs of scientists conducting experiments affect outcomes. The Schrödinger's cat thought experiment takes this a step further. It involves placing a

The principles of brain vs. mind, however, can be reduced to this: I have my mind and I have some of the brain I had then, only now that brain is not physical, and not in charge of anything except to control how I respond to things. The nonphysical neocortex exists without anything much else.

Logic is different now, as what I sense is there immediately, because I'm including in my experience the deeply held beliefs that I have always had. These are not <u>projected</u> as much as <u>continually uphold</u> my reality. In your world, control is more strongly worded as "I want that," then you go for it. Here there's not any need for that. We get what we desire, mostly, and everything else is just folly that we have no use for anymore.

So probabilities happen each time we breathe, in a sense, without the need to even think about them. You get the most real reality, therefore, that you can imagine, and that's what we do—<u>imagine</u>—all the time without really thinking too much about things.

Hence, I relate to you only in the sense of this shared environment of mind that we are finding to be expressed most wonderfully well in this phenomenon as you read. Who says we exist only as solo affairs

---

hypothetical cat in a hypothetical box with a device that has a 50-50 chance of killing the cat. Physicists have for decades used this imagined situation to discuss quantum physics. One interpretation is that <u>until the box is opened, the cat is both dead and alive</u> because the physical reality is not determined until the act of observation solidifies the probability into one state or another. In another interpretation, <u>both alive and dead states of the cat persist after the box is opened</u>.

when the world is spun round with many probable worlds being created all the time?

Each time you dream, each time you imagine, each time you say, "how about that?" you spin a probable world into existence. My world is no different than yours except that I have time for tea in the most inappropriate situations you might imagine.

The sense that you can use to determine the course of your life, therefore, has the sort of imaginative properties that require you to consider, then choose, one path or another. This is what I meant when I talked about the Infinite Probability Drive[46] in The *Hitchhiker's Guide to the Galaxy* books I wrote when I was physical.[47]

I was able to indicate in my books that the probabilities for something to happen are always going to come into play when they are required to. The sense of feeling into potentials that will happen at any given moment will come upon you. You may feel a bit

---

[46] This faster-than-light drive is based on the quantum theory that a subatomic particle can be in a location while there is also a probability of it being far from there, which connotes travel without passing through space. In Adams' words, "As the Improbability Drive reaches infinite improbability, it passes through every conceivable point in every conceivable universe almost simultaneously. In other words, you're never sure where you'll end up or even what species you'll be when you get there. It's therefore important to dress accordingly."

[47] Douglas added: "I'm still writing books, by the way. I just don't have them printed on paper. This is done through articulating, then responding to, where and when this can happen in physical reality. There are treatises being written by somebody physical who is tuning into me. However, that's another field of explanation I'll save for later."

of anxiety in the sense of "what potentials go where?" But you don't need to feel one way or another about them right away. Then you get a strong feeling, and then you go, "<u>Aha</u>! That's <u>it</u>!"

That's what's going on with me. That's what I've been thinking, and feeling, and trying to explain, even to myself: that the probability that you choose, the probability that may not even be part of your conscious effort to bring into reality, is the most real thing in the world. All the other probabilities—even the ones you don't take—<u>are real, too</u>. That's my point.

So what you might be thinking is, well, if I'm dead, then what about the self that's living now, happily ensconced in the Santa Barbara area eating bonbons and having a great old time writing my books? There's somebody there doing that now and yes, it is me. What you may not get fully yet is there's somebody else there doing that, who is living that life. The person there now <u>is</u> me, too, only different. In fact, he's me in the essence sense and not me in the purely physical sense. This has to do with how you define yourself as <u>self</u> or <u>Self</u>. The capitalization is intentional.

Do you feel the difference? Do you see how maybe there's a bigger "you" who is quite the charmer, who is you in a different way? Yes? Then you can understand how it is that you can be more than just yourself, the physical self. I'm me, I'm her, I'm you, I'm everybody who ever lived when you consider that probabilities don't need anybody saying "what's what" or "that's me" or not.

<u>The Universe is a probable, collective energetic pattern of existence that includes everybody in the</u>

world who ever lived. Is that the coolest thing you've ever heard?[48]

So when you talk about whether or not there's a God, probabilities help explain the reasons why you don't need to believe in God to understand the full picture: that everybody who ever lived is connected in some way to everybody who ever lived.

And in this, the spiritual dimension has to be included. That does not mean there's a God who sits on high judging everybody all the time. This means that He's us, period. And what matters is that we act like the blokes who want to bring goodness into the world, that's all. Because this is the point. To love really is the point. To just love and to allow oneself to believe in something greater than oneself, that's the point. Just don't necessarily consider this greater Self somebody who is all judge-y and mean when you piss him off.

That's what Richard and I were rebelling against: the idea that everything is run by this jerk. It's not. This whole thing seems to be run by love for one another,

---

[48] Rose explains probabilities in *The Way of Spirit:* "The way you can think of probabilities is that everything that can happen, will. This doesn't mean that you'll scratch your head in one scenario and in another you won't: it doesn't work to this degree of detail. Mostly, the probabilities of whether or not you will take a certain job or live in another place creates main sets of probabilities that serve as potential paths for you to take. … You have *probable selves* who experience certain probabilities that you don't, and they will experience certain paths sometimes, too. But in every case, they are you. While you can think of them as probable selves, keep in mind that they are real in every way — as real as you! You have the ability to see through their eyes at any time, as you sometimes do, for instance, in your dreams. This is yet another way to understand that you are part of a larger multidimensional being — your essence Self."

and that's why that fella who you like so much has such an important message: <u>to love one another</u>. What this doesn't mean is that you have to subscribe to one church or another. In fact, most churches resist this very basic idea, so some you can avoid entirely without missing out on anything that's beautiful.

When I was able, I had a heart attack. Now, you might see this as funny to say. However, at the time it was the weirdest thing I have ever been through. I was working out in the gym. I had a complete meltdown, so I laid down on a bench. I fought to keep myself awake. I had a heart attack. I clutched my towel to my chest and heaved a sigh of relief: <u>I had finally been able to accomplish this sendoff</u>!

Why? Because in my books, I wanted to impress on the reader that the situations in which one is prone to panic should be considered with a towel in hand. I was able to give myself the gift of the most poetic sendoff I could imagine, and had imagined it sometime along the way, I suppose. The act remains. I was able to give myself the most important gift, and that was a good death, really. Because there's nothing wrong with dying, it's what you do before and after that's important.

If you read my books, you will see that I was very much about transcendence in my own way. I was booked solid as a writer because of this. It was the kind of transcendence that comes from being able to brave the difficulty of life while proving oneself fit for love.

This was something I was able to represent well, if you ask me. I had enough backbone to see myself doing this, too. So when I died, I knew I had done a good job, and when I was able to move beyond where my body lie (by now I had fallen to the floor in the most awkward way possible), I was able to laugh at my circumstance and go forward without caring too much about what I had left behind.

I knew there was something to the afterlife only when I was in it, however, not before. The fact remained: there was someplace I needed to go next. What was it? Then I was surprised to find that there were people I knew there who welcomed me. This sounds odd coming from a self-described goddamned atheist. However, this was what happened.

Now what I want to tell you is, <u>you can still be an atheist and believe in the afterlife</u>. I was not going to see myself as anything except a rotting corpse until I was able to transcend the situation I found myself in, leaving my body in the locker room. When I was able to move forward (in a sense), I found many tears of joy running down my face because I was allowed to be with those I loved who had already passed. There were tears of solace, joy, mirth, everything that you can imagine was expressed in those moments.

The reason I say this is, emotion is key to humanness. We love emotions so much that we take them with us when we die. This is why I say we are human, which is what makes us eternal. Emotions are eternal, in a sense, and this relates to the notion I gave you about my ability to connect with the writer of this book. We share similar emotions and a sense of tuning into one another. So emotions are an important part of this whole thing.

And when I say I left as an atheist and am an atheist still, it's because who says anything is better than humanity? When humanity is at her best, of course. And why not share this information with others in ways that revoke the permissions for somebody to claim that God is the only one who is capable of doing such heavenly things?

I stress out thinking even now about the many individuals who have come into the world only to be total asses about what you are all supposed to do. I'm here to tell you: <u>don't feel bad</u>. If somebody makes you feel bad, it's only because you're buying into their bullshit. <u>Don't</u>!

What I want to say in conclusion is that this <u>is</u> going to end someday, and this is also **<u>not</u>** going to end someday. Don't feel you need to do anything special to enjoy your life. You can just allow yourself to enjoy yourself. I hope you do!

When you die, you can look me up and I will thank you for reading the works of both myself and Joanne, because you might notice there's a lot of me in her. But don't tell her. It'll spoil the surprise!

Best wishes,

Douglas Adams

CHAPTER 16

James Baldwin:
The Body is the Soul, the Soul the Body

The first time I saw a photo of James Baldwin, I fell in love with his face and displayed the photo on my computer desktop for a long time. I read about him but hadn't had a chance to read his books. Then one night Paul and I watched his 1965 debate with William F. Buckley, held at Cambridge University, England. I'll never forget Mr. Baldwin, a black man, surrounded by the "elite of the elite" young white men who packed the room to observe and vote on who would be the winner. The topic was whether the American dream had been achieved at the expense of African Americans. James Baldwin delivered a masterful rebuke of prevailing white elite perspectives. The student body voted overwhelmingly in Baldwin's favor.

James Baldwin (1924-1987) was an American novelist, essayist, playwright, poet, and activist. His work explores race, sexuality, and class differences in Western society, and parallels major social movements, including civil rights and gay liberation. Some of his work has been adapted for cinema as the Academy Award-nominated I Am Not Your Negro *and* If Beale Street Could Talk. *His work still speaks to our current challenges. "A civilization is not destroyed by wicked people; it is not necessary that people be wicked but only that they be spineless," he wrote in his bestselling essay,* The Fire Next Time.

When I was alive, the way I had of getting the attention of others was in my ability to be aware of what was going on with me and around me. The stressors of life were, for me, wonderful in the way they had of getting me to be aware of something, then I gave everything I had to the climate of scholarship as well as writing to become who I became, which was the writer and scholar James Baldwin.

The way in which I set to writing was to allow myself the complete freedom to say whatever it was that I wanted to say, which was from the very heart of my soul, if you can imagine that. This is where I'm speaking from now, from the depths of the heart of my soul, in the sense of my deepest self bringing to bear the deepest Self.

In this, I was going about the changes of life when I had my first insight into the nature of reality. The varied forms of life I observed held the complete and utter meaning of life for me in and of themselves. I was captivated by the world I lived in. The very people who were my friends were those that I loved more than anything.

This is still the same for me here, this is the same for me everywhere I go, and I don't let anybody tell me anything that I can't explain to them right back. I was always the one who had the most to say, therefore, and I want to shed some light on what I knew then and who I have grown into now.

Separate, if you will, the body from the soul in your very deep imagination. What is there, anyway? The soul has some elements to it that are different than the body, you might say. The body has elements of the soul, without all the seriousness that soul seems to elicit in our thoughts. Yet the body is the soul, the soul the body, and the course of history exemplifies this in its sheer abuses of body that wreck souls.

Do you follow? There are no different elements to body and soul. They are unique as well as the same. This is something that you can get used to thinking about before you move into the world I inhabit now, the ideas around the soul being body and the body being soul.

When has this idea ever not existed?

When somebody tries to pull you into a situation in which you are left grieving for the world's problems, this is when you say to yourself, "This can't be, this physical thing with this horror happening. Where is the soul in all this?" <u>The soul is there</u>. You don't see it because you don't believe the soul <u>is</u> body.

Now when you characterize soul as body, you see how very large the soul is. Exactly where does the soul leave off from body to body? It doesn't: the soul remains locked <u>in</u> body <u>from</u> body <u>to</u> body <u>forever</u>. And the body type will change: the souls will alter it to express the kinds of things you know will need to be expressed. But you double down on your body so you can see yourselves as different, when the reality is, you're not. <u>You're One Body, you're One Soul, and you're quite likely to appreciate life more when you discover this</u>.

This is the hope for the future. The torrents of racial injustice and inequality due to the differences of body will have their day for some more years. Then you will notice how each person you meet has some of your soul in them, some of your body in their body, and you will finally recognize the utility of the expressions of *unum corpus* that transcends the narrowness you find yourselves in each day when you consider yourselves separate from each other and the world around you.

Now, in your lives you have a lot of things going on that are not exactly moving you into where you need to be. The primary reasons are that you don't yet realize that you're not separate or unequal and you want to strive to be better than others, to be more beautiful than you perhaps ever have been. Realize, though, this is folly, for you will never be anything different than the whole thing. The way to view this is as another kind of sense: <u>the sense of being part of the greater reality</u>.

Your path will show you where to go, and it will show you everybody you have realized as Selfhood in other body form. That's how you can consider yourselves now, tumbling into the twenty-first century without a life preserver, tossed about like a bottle on the waves, full of nature and envy and clouds of distrust. Break the bottle and allow yourselves the best gift you can give yourselves: the freedom to melt into the grander oceans of your reality and allow this to take you into the beautiful new lives you have awaiting you.

This is the way I moved through my own death experience, by considering myself tossed through an ocean without needing to hold onto anything except the sense of beauty I have experienced while on my journey. This is what I noticed: bright lights, shared feelings with someone else (I don't know who this was — the feelings were <u>personal</u>, deeply so, but not attributable to a specific <u>person</u>), the elegance of my form, and the mind I had grown used to, now expanding into a sort of multiverse of ideas I'd not realized before, the sense of power as well as weakness at the same time, more of a cleansing perhaps than anything, without worrying about what would be left.

This was what was left: an awareness of sentience in myself as well as everything around me, which was laid out like an elegant, grace-filled journey with no markers for help along the way. There was a trust in the journey. This is all I recall now, which is a lot, given I'm more grounded now in my afterdeath environment.

Now I read, I lecture, I have friends, lovers, everything that I want here, without needing to feel lacking of anything I missed. The stories are funnier, the games more or less the same only not at all painful in the sense of the political scene, which of course there is one.

For example, each time you [Joanne] ask another person to write through you, there's a political situation that presents itself, a kind of jockeying for time with you that's not quite mean, just somewhat aggressive, believe it or not. The Committee sheds light on who should go next, and this is what I mean by One Body, because we're in charge of ourselves here, and we have the common sense that the best minds will prevail. What you don't see now with each author is we're all here with you now.

We're around you now without your seeing us, with another kind of journey in front of all of us, which is the publication of this book. The journey, the probability of it being a big success, excites us. You can't even imagine how much that excites all of us, because we want to assist people in their lives, and how else will they know to ask us if they don't realize we're here any time to help? The readers who explore these ideas, even these few words, allow us to feel them quite remarkably close and to help them through their own intuitions and insights.

The reason we are doing this, therefore, is to enjoy ourselves without need to feel that we can do more to help. And that's why we do what we do each day, spurring you—each of you—on in your thoughts, at times teaching you through your books that we write, and enjoying your stories, too, as they unfold without our intervention, however with complete interest on our part.

The path for you is going to be wonderful. We see this and we stress again how very much we want to help you. Let us!

With the very best regards you can imagine,

James Baldwin

CHAPTER 17

Kurt Vonnegut, Jr.:
Just Say Vonnegut Sent You

I was stunned by James Baldwin's chapter, especially when he described how much the authors want to come through. I was still having trouble getting my head around it. I have the worst kind of imposter syndrome, as even what I do is considered fraudulent — even pathological and heretical — by many. Sadly, some of those people are my friends and family, which is why getting the authors' encouragement is so valuable. Baldwin said, "The journey, the probability of it being a big success, excites us." I was excited, too, but didn't think "big success" was likely. I'd never had an agent or publisher, so my books had not reached many people, and while my new dead author friends said they'd help, I didn't know how they could. So I continued to focus on what was in my control: ensuring the authors were accurately given voice and loving this book into the world.

I had a few authors in mind to invite next, including Vonnegut, who I read a lot of in my teens. Paul had given me a large photo of him, which I had on the wall next to my desk. One day, I looked at the photo and caught him staring at me, so I figured I'd better get on with it.

Kurt Vonnegut Jr. (1922-2007) was an American writer of novels, short stories, plays, and nonfiction. He is most famous for his novel **Slaughterhouse-Five,** *which calls on his experiences as an American prisoner of war who survived the horrific firebombing of Dresden, Germany, in February 1945. Michael Crichton noted that Vonnegut* *"writes about the most excruciatingly painful things. His novels have attacked our deepest fears of automation and the bomb, our deepest political guilts, our fiercest hatreds and loves. No one else writes books on these subjects; they are inaccessible to normal novelists."*

Vonnegut, who once described himself as a "Christ-loving atheist," seems to have intuited the afterlife in Slaughterhouse-Five. *In it, the protagonist travels to the fictitious planet Tralfamador, where there is only simultaneous time. He notes: "The most important thing I learned on Tralfamadore was that when a person dies he only appears to die. He is still very much alive in the past, so it is very silly for people to cry at his funeral. All moments, past, present and future, always have existed, always will exist."*

I don't have anything else to say except what I said when I was physical, in the chair I sat in day after day, contemplating the things I thought were important. The Soviet plague. The leaders who sell their souls for money. The exclusion of most people from reaching the goals they set most beautifully. The commerce that excludes everybody without a buck. Each of these challenges <u>still</u> live in your world. I don't know what else I can say about them, so I will say pretty much what I said when I was physical.

Looking back, I would have preferred to not be another writer who said things that people enjoyed reading about. This kind of writer only has so many words to say without a lot of influence, ultimately. Will and patience were not my strong suits, so I would not have gone too readily into public service in the sense of just showing up for some job every day. I had to let myself enjoy my work, and this was the best I could do. Still, I don't know for sure how many people's lives were improved by the books or short stories I wrote. I don't think they were influenced much at all, frankly.

I <u>do</u> believe, though, that they enjoyed knowing there was somebody who really needed to say what was being said, and that they were in total agreement with it. This way, they did not feel so alone in thinking what they thought to be different than the status quo. Therefore, I think the best thing I can say for my work is that it helped people feel better about the fucked up world they live in.

Now, this is not entirely the case, of course. There are many beautiful things about the world, okay? I get that, yes. And there are many beautiful things about life that are to be enjoyed fully. However, if you only consider those things as the things that are important, you will be missing about ninety percent of what the world really is about.

The world suffers greatly. The earth is not going to last much longer, all things going as they are. The moon will be okay as long as you can stop everybody from destroying it with their lasers and robots. The world will continue in this way for the foreseeable future, on the most part. However, the work being done now will soon be helpful to more people. That's a good thing.

However, you have so many people in charge of rotten establishments that pretend to help and don't, that you really need to do something about it. That's what I did. However, you can do even better than I did because here's what's really going on today.

You're blooming! See how I did that? I went directly from one fucked up world of rotten men and turned it to something that you can readily see as true.

You're blooming, and you're intuiting the things that I did when physical that really will make for a better world. Ways in which people can see each other as family. Ways in which science can be used to promote larger views of reality. And the kinds of servant minds that are needed. You see this each day in your newspapers and television sets.

The people who are servants will, of course, be the ones who will be held in the highest esteem by those who know better. And you of all people should know what the deal is with yourself because you have the servant mind in you, too. You have the application of goodness and reason, and articulation of the best kinds of ideas that you would ever want to see happen in the world.

So, when you can, try to view yourselves as the black humor doctors of the world. Or the science fiction seers. Or the lost cause lovers who find their satisfaction in helping the long shots that won't make it anyway.

What about this makes your heart sing? If you could do anything at all, would you go forth like a prince on a steed, there to wed the princess and inherit the castle? Or will you take up arms to defend your masses of terror-filled refugees who die every day wanting to escape the hell of their homelands? Will you save the ragged, wretched animals from despairing lives, unloved and unwanted? What about the people, dear people?

Would you at least recognize that the world is pretty fucked up and do something — anything you can — to help?

I again have to say I wasn't the best person to do the work I did. I wasn't the most civil or inviting of humor all the time, either. I was an aging drunk with love for the world, a superstar author who had not any reason to feel he'd done any good in the world.

I don't want you to feel that way. I want you to be a force of Nature that sheds whatever kind of pride or fear you have to do the very best goddamned job you can, whatever your field of study or area of expertise. Do what you can! Have fun doing it, if you can, and speak loudly to anyone who will hear you: "<u>Goddammit, this has to change!</u>"

Then do it, because God Almighty is on your side, and all of us here, and you will see through the wreckage of your lives in ways that are spectacular. You will see how your life has been totally suited for you now that you're on your way to being a superhero who will call on every misdeed, every regret, every forbidden thought, to enjoy the kind of life that lets you help others.

And when you do, you can say for sure that Vonnegut sent you.

That's all. Just say Vonnegut sent you.

With extreme gratitude for the opportunity to sermonize on this fine day here on Planet Tralfamadore,

Kurt Vonnegut, Jr.

CHAPTER 18

Aldous Huxley:
Just Go Along for the Ride

I felt I could go on forever channeling dead people, but the book needed to end at some point. It also needed a title. So I asked the Committee for their input on this proposed title, Afterlives: Firsthand Accounts of Twenty Notable People, *and anything else they wanted to share.*

The Committee: We think the title is excellent and we will help with the final chapters. The reason for wanting to do the book is to break new ground in the world. We think this is happening now with regard to your work and ours, so don't be afraid of those who will try to discredit you.

The reason we are doing this is to help ensure your credibility as well as ours. And we will do what we can to ensure that those who have helped complete the book have their say about what to expect in the world as a result of writing it. We want to see you thriving in the next phase as a writer — as we have — and to be in the world in ways we have often enjoyed. So join us in this legion of authors, dear one. We love you.

There were three chapters to go. Paul, who had abstained thus far from suggesting anyone, requested Aldous Huxley, a good choice! We'd both recently read his book Island *and have for many years been inspired by his quote illustrating the need for integral approaches to the systemic challenges we face.*

Science is not enough, religion is not enough, art is not enough, politics and economics is not enough, nor is love, nor is duty, nor is action however disinterested, nor, however sublime, is contemplation. Nothing short of everything will really do.

Aldous Huxley (1894-1963) was an English author and one of the most notable thinkers of his time. His interest in philosophical mysticism influenced his works including The Perennial Philosophy, *which describes commonalities between Western and Eastern mysticism, and* The Doors of Perception, *which explores the hallucinogenic effects of mescaline. He was a prominent advocate for the responsible use of psychedelics, including psilocybin, the active ingredient in magic mushrooms. His most famous novel,* Brave New World, *presents a dystopian vision of a society whose scientific advancements have conditioned citizens towards conformity, consumerism, and instant gratification, depriving them of a sense of purpose and happiness.*

The promise of tomorrow is something I have always been interested in, without getting too involved in the world myself. I was calm when I was alone writing, not so much when I was in the world being social. Having fun with groups of friends was something I wasn't always drawn to. So I think the completion of books can be rather trying, as the writing is so very different than the promoting. That was something I didn't like much. However, it will help to have a calling forth of friendly ghosts to help you through it. This will be my submission for the book. My name is Aldous Huxley.

Beginning with my first reports I made of school goings-on, I was reporting from my perspective as somebody who was not happy with how things tended to go. I saw too much abuse, too much conjecture with regard to the truth of things, too many people with their hands slapped for the slightest transgressions. I was wounded to the core by those saying that the world would never change or have any reason to change, either, which for me was horrible to hear.

Still, I was not going to take this as rote. I was going to look into the world of psilocybin mushrooms and other tasty medicines for my own natural explorations of what reality <u>really</u> is, and if you can see yourself as somebody who's also experimenting with alternate reality, you will get a taste of what I have experienced. This doesn't really need to be induced by medicines such as LSD, although these were helpful for me. This can also be done by the sheer openness to subtle energies around you.

This is what my trips were doing—helping me sense what was around me all the time—and I was able to progress into a sort of hallucinatory state even when I was not tripping. This was only because I was open, not because I perceived any differently than most people. In fact, I think most people just turn things off because they want to, or they think they're supplied[49]

---

[49] I checked to see if the word was to be "supposed" but it wasn't. I asked Huxley for an explanation. "The word 'supplied' often has a context in which objects of life are provided to subjects in order to support special functions, in this case, being robots. In this, the characteristics of provisions are enough food, shelter, and common things necessary to support an automaton, which humans are not. The characteristics of provisions for humans

to live in the world as robots, doing what they do without questioning things.

That's why I wrote what I wrote, and I did what I did, because life was too wonderful in the stratosphere of the world of ideas in my own imagination that I was able to poke through to reach those in need of my perspectives. This made a difference in the world, and I was able to also expand myself upon reaching this "state of environment" that I'm in now. The state of environment is what I call this because it's not quite <u>real</u>, not quite <u>unreal</u>, yet totally worthy of description, which I will attempt to do now.

This environment—this world of ideas I can only describe as a "state"—is likely something you will feel comfortable with if you have the kind of vivid imagination that some people have. This isn't the best way to describe it, though, as the significance goes far beyond what you think of as folly, sometimes—what the imagination cooks up. However, that folly is not here, really. The folly is in thinking that the prescription for being in heaven is to be somewhat of a false person with only the benefit of twenty-twenty hindsight to show you otherwise.

Do you follow? The cooking up of a good life is sometimes not what you think it is, because the tantamount thing to realize is that you don't need to live by anyone else's rules besides your own. The reason I say this is because the rules are what help you realize this state of environment you will go into sometimes, too. The rejections, the falsehoods—these

include intellectual pursuits, caring pursuits, and other forms of greater Selfhood that are what needs to be supplied for full human development."

are not at all important. The important things are to realize you have nothing to do with heaven or hell, you only have to do with what you think the rules are.

The reason is that the rules are what create your reality here. So "investigating fun things that interest you" is a rule you might have to work on if you have only experienced small degrees of latitude with regard to what you think is right living. Expressions of guilt will be unnecessary here, although you might take some of the guilt with you, but you will let go of that eventually.

The potentials for whatever it is you want to see or do, therefore, are <u>limitless</u>! You only need to be open to what you want to discover or explore. The reason this is necessary is, you will have done the work on being human. Next, you will be able to become human <u>beyond</u> human without caring overly much about what the world thinks about you.

What a grand way to go about living after you have not only shed the body but also the unnecessary limits to your own thinking. *Brave New World* was about that. The necessary things of life will not ever be about what you do with yourself, in the sense of needing to show off, or expend great amounts of energy being liked or appreciated. No, the brave new world is about trusting yourselves to be who you need to be in order to adjust the world towards goodness: indeed, to greatness.

In my books, I was able to create a sort of alternate reality through fiction. The *Brave New World* book was rightly called this because the brave will be the ones who get to where you need to go next as evolution progresses. Brave is not the term that you might consider the same as courageous, however. Brave in my sense of the word is more about being able to dispose of those things that don't do anything for you or your lives. Disposing of care for what others consider important or frivolous that you don't. Disposing of things that make you sad or feel rejection. Things that are not as able to spell out what you think about the world like your home does: it shares you in the world.

Why not allow this ache of your heart to get past its own fears and be bravely making life the way you want it to be, rather than what you think it is, now?

That's what my books were trying to get at, I suppose, with some allowance for credit. This was not entirely my world. The world was not entirely my world. My world was more a self-made, congenial place of exposure to ideas that served my interests.

This is what you do each day when you settle into a kind of hypnotic state, enjoying your thinking state rather than directing it. The path of your imagination will take you to the kinds of places that are wonderful, mostly. Sometimes you will encounter fears of things you haven't yet figured out are not in need of fearing, and you will get past the clamor of thinking when you realize this is going exactly the way it's supposed to go. For when you encounter anything, you can just ride along with it without fear or mistrust of where the journey is taking you: <u>just go along for the ride</u>.

The distortions and misunderstandings of psychedelic experiences have made an entire generation lost in the post-World War II era to lose out also on the very medicine that would help them. This fear of aggravated experiences has cost you dearly in how you might have healed the world. However, the attempts now to corroborate scientific data on the use of psychotropic enhancements, even in small quantities, are useful now, even as we write this. The future will hold many more therapeutic options.

For now, realize there's not any reason to fear this brand of science. In every case, the scientists realize, too, that the brain needs companionship on the way, and guided trips will begin to be the norm as soon as you realize this is a need for everyone who is beginning on their journey. The trips can be expressed in terms of high quality, as well as medium quality, as long as they are induced by helpers to guide you through what might be a tough spot.

The reason we're going into this kind of thinking is to help you realize this will be okay in the future. The transference of fear to love is part of your effort to help the people of your world take better care of themselves and their lives. There's no need for war. There's no need for abolishing the things that people need — such as fair pay and a say in their governance — for fear they will rise up. What constitutes the future, therefore, is based in your own experiences as goodness, as pleasure, in the depth of your being.

Remarkably, the world will allow you the widest advantage in expressing yourselves. We — the essence of Aldous Huxley, as well as his own benevolent presence — suggest you do so.

With great love and affection for the world,

Aldous Huxley

CHAPTER 19

Robin Williams:
Chairman of the Board

Two chapters to go! Having this book completed in the final days of the trying year of 2020 would be a great big bright spot. I had some authors in mind, but was reluctant to choose, as I felt bad for the ones who wouldn't make it into the book. I didn't want to hurt anyone's feelings. I'd wanted to speak to Robin after his suicide in 2014, but didn't, so it felt right to me that he be next.

Robin Williams (1951-2014) was an American actor, comedian, and philanthropist. His rapid-fire improvisational stand-up routines included his personal issues such as depression and drug and alcohol addiction. He went on to star in many successful films and won many awards. Williams had been sober but severely depressed before his death. His suicide was attributed to his struggle with Lewy body disease, a progressive dementia that effects the nerve cells in the brain regions involved in thinking, memory, and motor control. Beloved by many, his death was a shock. President Barack Obama released a statement upon Williams' death that reminded us of his many acting roles:

Robin Williams was an airman, a doctor, a genie, a nanny, a president, a professor, a bangarang Peter Pan, and everything in between ... He arrived in our lives as an alien — but he ended up touching every element of the human spirit. He made us laugh. He made us cry. He gave his immeasurable talent freely and generously to those who needed it most—from our troops stationed abroad to the marginalized on our own streets.

Ladies and gentlemen, I present Robin Williams.

I didn't have the common decency to expect to live for anybody else at the time of my departure, so I do regret doing what I did. What I did—death by suicide—was the act of an extremely desperate man who saw only suffering ahead for himself. On second thought—which I have had so many of, into the millions of second thoughts—I've begun finally to climb out of the morass of emotion that I had to work through when I first became nonphysical.

The temptations of actors are numerous. These include the sorts of inspired concoctions of drugs that were plenty during the time of my stage work. Then and now, there is great temptation to do the things that eventually will indeed make you crazy. I did not go crazy. I was <u>already</u> crazy in my own way, <u>crazy good</u> in the sense of being funny and having the kind of imagination that took me where I wanted to go. The days I spent acting were the best days of my life.

I couldn't comprehend at the time the effects the drugs had on my body, or my soul, for that matter. The effects were physical sleeplessness, erratic behavior— not to mention depression—that go along with some of them. These were only bodily effects for me, not soul ones, and I was only looking out after my body in the end. The soul was something to look forward to, not really as much a part of me, or so I thought—merely something to take care of everything without engaging me much.

Therefore, the desperation that occurred when I was older and portly, for me, was that I was going downward fast without any instructions from soul about what to do with myself except die.

The effects of the drugs complicated the neurotransmitters of my brain that stimulated organs in my body in ways that perfectly demonstrated how to create an ailing old man. This old man was not somebody I wanted to be, and I was in serious agony, body-wise. Mind-wise, too. I had not really prepared myself for the final outcome. Hence, there was a lot of processing to do when I became nonphysical.

The trials of life were, therefore, complicated by my drug use. This was not something I was proud of, however. The side effects should warn you into not doing them, frankly.

Was there a real reason I needed to do them? Not really. They were fun, they kept me awake, they made me manic sometimes, and that was what my brand was built upon. However, in the end, I don't think I needed them to become what I became, which was an accomplished actor, and I'm proud of that. This was something I had chosen foremost as my profession. The comedy was just a start. This was complicated by family woes, though I'm especially proud of my children, who I love to this day, and I'm with them more than they know.

So where am I now?

Knowing what I know about how this [channeling] work is accomplished, I can say without question that I have the kind of ultimate effect as somebody who whispers rather than yells, as I did when on comedy stages. I whisper all the time now. I was getting that way in the end—whispering, that is—and I needed to calm down in order to be heard.

Quite reasonable, don't you think? There's whispering in physical reality, there's whispering in nonphysical reality, which is where I'm at now, and the whispering happens all the time, you just need to listen.

There were appointments made to the Non-Physically Adept HOA Board[50] where I live, appointments to see this book through. I was asked to be in charge of the book in a Chairman of the Board kind of way because I had so many reasons to want to do it. Therefore, I was able to convince them that I would do the job, and this book has been helpful in getting me centered on a goal that I would have fun doing. So let me explain to you how this is possible.

You know me as somebody who was funny and smart, right? Now, I'm more than Robin. I'm now something of an oversoul who was able to go so far in his healing that I incorporated massive amounts of energy, the kind of energy I had when I was in charge of the cocaine stash. I was bearing many kinds of agonies of the soul, however. In this, I was able to accomplish <u>much</u> in the afterlife.

What kinds of things was I able to move through? Well, use your imagination. Without naming names, do you think I worked with the brightest and smartest actors and entertainers? Yes I did. So you can imagine, then, how very boisterous it gets here—this nonphysical planet we're on—when we get together.

---

[50] HOA is the acronym for Home Owners Association, the typical governing body of a suburban neighborhood that is run by an elected Board of Trustees.

The facts of heaven are that you go as you, primarily, then you heal, then you become <u>more than you</u>. With my ability to channel the many kinds of personas through my own work, I was fit for doing the kind of "integration of my parts" in the soul sense, to help me include more Selfhood than before. There were a lot of aspects to me. Each time I played a role in a movie, for example, some part of me was formed or shaped, and this became useful in my ability to include more soul, in a sense, after I became nonphysical.

So when you consider how you blend together psychologically as people even now, then consider how rapt you are reading these words typed by somebody who isn't the person saying the words, you get a sense of how integrated people really are. And you get a sense they will be even more integrated beyond your physical world. So what seems like chaos in your physical world is merely the camouflage that's required to hide the worlds beyond, so you may enjoy the incredible kinds of experiences you have here on Planet Earth.

Do you follow this? I'm the Chairman of the Board who's overseen how this book's been written, along with numerous other people who have the power to move people in ways they need to be moved. For me to deny my presence in helping this work along would be selfish. The unfolding of each authentic transmission from nonphysical to physical has everything to do with <u>cooperation</u>.

Therefore, when your writer here says she doesn't want to hurt anybody's feelings, she doesn't need to fear that. She knows deep down that whatever comes through is what needs to come through for everybody including you, her, and us. So we don't have the kind of aggressive stance that you might think we do, given how you feel about people sometimes. We <u>do</u> assert ourselves, which is why James [Baldwin] said what he said[51]. However, the point is to get past the idolatry of ego into a more stable, fair, and helpful collaboration between artists.

Isn't that the most wonderful thing you can imagine? You are witnessing this now in the ever-present, wondrous creation that you have found in these pages, as well as in the incredible, grace-filled moments that elude you sometimes without your needing to even pay attention. That's our job — to help realize these grace-filled moments of transcendence. And we do this with whispering.

This is all you need to do: <u>just pay attention to the whispers from those who love you each day</u>. When you least expect this, you will hear us. We promise!

May I comment? I understand that Robin may have assimilated a lot of Rose energy, and maybe always did. But I'm not sure this rings true for people like me who expect more of the Robin who was grounded in physical reality — the man we felt we knew.

---

[51] He's referencing James Baldwin's comment in Chapter 17: "Each time you ask another person to write through you, for example, there's a political situation that presents itself, and there's another kind of jockeying for time with you that's not quite mean, just somewhat aggressive, believe it or not. The Committee sheds light on who should go next, and this is what I mean by One Body, because we're in charge of ourselves here, and we have the common sense the best minds will prevail."

I'm getting to that, so please bear with me, beautiful. This is a lengthy chapter because I needed to establish myself as who I am now, in addition to the person I was. So hang on, that's coming up.

We, therefore, were not always this version of ourselves — us members of the Committee which is ruled by the greater Self that is *moi*, my own version of Robin Williams, now expanded into the kind of benign dictator that I always wanted to be. We were who you knew us as, the delightful characters, artists, and providing-of-love writers who you know and love. We are still that, depending on how you think of us. But we're that and more now. The point is, this is all happening at the same time — you with Robin, Robin with the Committee, the Committee with the greater collective of persons who ever were — all of it working together.

The point of this lengthy diatribe is that <u>we didn't get here by being wonderful all the time</u>. We got here by being terribly hurt sometimes, terribly hurting others sometimes, and grandly fucking up our lives sometimes. That's the point.

Now let me tell you more about who I was when I was alive with you. Some of you knew me as the person who was totally in the moment, contacting unseen elements of imagination in his ability to profoundly address the scene at the time, the actor who was able to conjure the deepest sympathies from others, and the most lamentable druggie in the Vale of Tears[52] known as Hollywood. I was all that, yes. I was

---

[52] "Vale of tears" is a Biblical phrase that refers to the difficulties of life that are left behind when one leaves the world and enters heaven.

able to do more with my body, mind, and spirit than most people. When I got down, I was able to take something. I was able to take more of something than I needed. Then I was able to douse myself with alcohol and other libations to end the suffering I had in my heart, the kind of suffering that only sensitive people know.

When I was able, I was enjoying myself immensely, but the pain remained. I was truly another kind of person, a sensitive melancholic who was not ever really able to transcend the suffering of the world.

Now, you know people like this. They tend to be up a lot, tend to be nervous at times, and fidgety, maybe. They are sympathetic listeners. They are also the kind of people who take things in deeply, effortlessly creating the kinds of worries about everything that occlude their own safety at times. This was me. Then you have very many people like this who trouble themselves with troubles and don't know what to do to end the suffering. This was me then, and it's me now, too.

Why is it both now? Do you think that I would have abandoned this person because I've grown up to be the Chairman of the Board? No, that's the point here. I'm that way now, too, only in another kind of realm where I have collected these wonderful attributes of Selfhood. I can't be the Chairman of the Board without this sad little suicidal maniac who I was, and love now more than anything, perhaps. I'm <u>more</u> than him, yet I'm <u>still</u> him, too.

What would your requirements be for a Chairman of the Board who would guide this kind of thing? Would you want them to be mean, cruel, or dishonest?

No, you would want him to be like Robin was — kind, generous, suffering his own woes with dignity. He is and was somebody who you want in your corner. Therefore, he's also the Chairman of the Board.

When you see people laughing, you have the kind of response that says, "that's good, that's acceptable." That eases your suffering. And yet sometimes the laughter is covering up a multitude of errors in thinking, for example, that the life you have is not worthy of your own satisfaction. The laughter may cover up an emotion that you can't face, or a reality you can't share with somebody.

The laughter is important, yes. However, beware the laughter sometimes. It will hide a multitude of suffering. But rather than stop laughing, consider looking deeper at the smiles and the antics of somebody who is doing whatever he or she can to get the joy of life into your atmosphere, because nine times out of ten, it's because they are suffering and want to help you not to suffer.

Then what can you expect this to be, other than a sacrifice of personal suffering for the benefit of others? What more can you desire from your own experiences than somebody who knocked himself out to join up with the Gods to create the kinds of love and laughter for those who are also suffering? What do you call this person? You call them Christ. You call them the Messiah. You call them your Savior, and they <u>are</u>.

Do you see? What more valid experience would you ever hope to invent than somebody relieving somebody else's sorrow by sacrificing their own? In this, Robin wasn't just a comedian or actor. <u>He was a goddamned Savior</u>. And you can use him as an example for yourselves and others, because there's nothing more beautiful than that.

Try to emulate him, but don't try to suffer in the way he did. You don't need to. Try to give of yourselves to the most profound degree that you can, then allow the most beautiful, selfless acts to follow. You will have the most exquisite lives you can imagine. From the world of laughter and love will come the most beautiful effects on your world that you can imagine.

Now we want to say just one more thing about this, and that is yes, we're here with you all the time. Yes, you have gotten that from the other writers here. What you don't really get yet is that we don't play hide and seek. We're there all the time, whether you're undressed or not. We know this is a question you've had, so we'll address this now.

The things you want to remember about a person aren't what they looked like on the toilet or only wearing their underpants. The things you want to remember about people is that which transcends these common daily experiences that we don't have any interest in.

Therefore, don't worry about these things when considering us near you. We're here remembering you as wonderful. And in remembering all of your strengths and different kinds of beauty, the rest falls away like your underpants reaching the floor as you sit to do your business.

With lovingkindness from the far corners of the Galaxy we send our love and laughter,

Robin Williams, Chairman of the Board

CHAPTER 20

Jane Roberts:
Dream On, Dear Humans

I write this on the last day of 2020, a year in which a global pandemic turned our fragile world upside down. Last week, on Christmas Day, the Great Conjunction of Jupiter and Saturn occurred, creating a bright, starlike presence in the night sky. Astrologers say it signals a great shift in consciousness. What timelier message than Robin's suggestion in the previous chapter that we can all be Saviors simply by serving one another? Perhaps this Christmas star represents our own rebirth as better versions of ourselves and our species.

I feel the best person for ending this book is the one who began it – Jane Roberts – my teacher and role model. She's had a profound influence on millions of people who never knew her in physical reality, which is poetic, given the nature of her profound gifts. She brought in an era in which channeling became mainstream and paved the way for the writing of this book and others like it.

Jane Roberts (1929-1984) was an American poet, author, and psychic who channeled the energy personality essence Seth. Jane's husband, Robert Butts, was a critical part of the work, providing sanity and support as he transcribed by hand all of the information that Jane delivered in trance state. Part of the Seth Material's appeal is the journey of Jane and Rob from their initial skepticism of extrasensory perception to the publication of over forty books, some written by Seth and some by Jane. The Seth Material is housed in the Yale University Library.

I can't begin to tell you how grateful I am to be part of the writing of this book. My many reasons to do so involve my life and my origins as a psychic.

The purpose of my life was to incorporate in my body, mind, and spiritual overview[53] the presence of "other." The background I had was necessary to contrive the kind of life that enabled me to do this. I was born poor to a mother who was in every way possessed by a kind of sadness that affected her nervous system. It caused her much suffering, and I was the only one who was there to support her. Therefore, my childhood was solitary for the most part, except for my mother, who I cared for.[54]

The reason I say "solitary" is because I was not truly gifted in the way of words — when talking, that is. I was gifted in writing, and my writing began early, even before I could write, in a sense, because I was able to develop my thoughts in curious ways — by solitude and loneliness sometimes, too. Therefore, when the local priests were able to stop by to visit, I had a rich sense of possibility, and this led me to include in my thinking the ideas about God they had. Their God was a singular kind of person — a man, of course — who had to try better at helping people, so he created a Savior —

---

[53] I asked Jane what she meant by "spiritual overview." She said: "I don't like the term 'spiritual' or 'spirit' so much. These tend to weigh down the very reciprocity of spirit in the world of physicality. 'Spiritual overview' is more of an energetic feeling of spirit that I include in my intellectual capability as well."

[54] This is a kind way to say it. Jane's mother — who was bedridden with rheumatoid arthritis — was abusive, and the responsibility of Jane, a child, to care for. Jane was also bedridden with severe arthritis for the year and a half prior to her death.

a son—to come to the earth to help spread love and helpfulness to the world.

I had to take in the lessons of their doctrines because that was how they worked, you know. Without needing to go into detail, there was a lot of suffering involved in the teachings of the Catholics. So the suffering part was not exactly right, in my view now, as the suffering wasn't necessary for Saviorship. This was something that did stick with me, though. I had to immerse myself in my life without sinning, of course, and that was also suspect. The Blessed Mother was considered a virgin when she gave birth to Jesus, and that was something that was mostly believed by rote, although I had my own suspicions about this even at an early age.

The qualifications for Christhood were the ones that held me in their thrall. The qualifications were those that had Jesus being brotherly most of the time, and angry sometimes, questioning the authorities sometimes. That was all fine with me. The suffering, though, was something I wasn't able to fully get on board with. This was the fact, though, of my life—I suffered a lot—but the suffering was not going to be given away for free. The suffering, therefore, had to do with <u>how</u> you suffered, <u>why</u> you suffered, and if the suffering was truly the thing necessary to live, then I would do it as long as it was for a good cause.

The reason I'm going into this detail is because this fit the framework of my life, the way I, as an oversoul that you might also call essence, saw how I would navigate the world of ideas.[55]

---

[55] The term "oversoul" is common to many spiritual works and denotes a united essence of various souls into one that transcends and includes them all. Jane is talking about her own essence here

I was able to put aside all this when I became a grownup and spent miraculous days sorting through the world of ideas, not only the ones I was raised with. I read extensively the works of Emerson, Thoreau, and others who had wider views, in my opinion, than those of the Catholics, and I had to bridge some gaps in my understanding of the Christ figure. I was able to see him for who he is—in my view still—as somebody who was persecuted for who he was, a sentient being gifted in the precognitive and other psychic kinds of abilities that most people don't really pay attention to.

We here—all of us that are writing this book—have a greater sense about who he was because we are that now. We have the ability to see into the way things are, the way things were, and the way things ought to be. If you have the ability to perceive greater energies, you will see a better future. The Christ information is central to this occurring, and to set the record straight is something we're all interested in, ultimately.

The Christ figure you knew was not somebody who persecuted anybody or condemned anyone. We see him as the being of Light that you become when you see yourselves this way. The reason we have for spending time on the Christ figure is because you have to update your ideas about him and who he was, to egg yourselves onto creating a better world.

That kind of suffering, therefore, is part of the myth that we want to dispel. You suffer daily with the things of the world, the things that make your world hard to

---

which, like each of our own essences, chooses our physical lifetimes.

be in. The suffering is there. However, to take on any suffering in order to free yourselves is not needed.

This is what I learned when physical. I was capable of doing what I did, enchanting my readers with the Seth Material, gaining notoriety with my books while spending countless hours in pain with rheumatoid arthritis. The "sinful self" ideas found in the Seth information[56] exquisitely portray the issues I had, and that suffering was <u>not</u> needed. The work could have been done without it. The suffering was included in my thinking because I thought it needed to be.

Therefore, we want you to let go of any ideas you have about Saviors needing to be persecuted or to die suffering. These are not necessarily the ways to go if you will take on the idea of being a <u>servant savior</u> — not a heroic, damaging one, but a truly gifted, humble servant of the world. You don't need to die for your cause. You don't need to even give up your wealth. You only need to commit to doing everything you can to help the world, not at the expense of your own lives but as providers of necessary things to others. Sacrifices will need to happen sometimes, but ultimately, you're better alive in the world than you are dead.

The surface-level teachings, therefore, hide the inner reality that I strove to publish in the Seth Material. These books are waiting for you to discover and read, so we won't go into too much detail. What

---

[56] The "sinful self" is a term Seth used to describe "many unfavorable concepts that are held by the various religions — concepts that certainly make many people feel that the self is indeed sinful rather than blessed. The self is indeed blessed, and just the reminder of that fact can often short-circuit negative beliefs." – Jane Roberts/Seth, *The Way Toward Health*

we strive for is to assist others in understanding their own calling, or need for peace, in their own lives. Following the call of one's heart is something that brings peace each day, and this is necessary for you as well as for the world.

Now, I had a rough start to life, perhaps, but my misery was ended when I married Robbie Butts. He was the light of my life who also served as transcriber of the material, as well as publisher if you include the important work of typing pages for supplying to the books' publishers.

I had to wait anxiously for the books to come out. I had to sacrifice my own comfort for the understanding that the books might cause a stir, given their antithetical nature towards the commanding presence of the Church. However, this was the sacrifice needed.

See what I mean? You sometimes have to let go of whatever you need to in order to sacrifice for your Greater Self, too: the Self that's waiting for you in the ability to do something unselfish. The path for me was loaded with insecurities about who I was as an artist, who I was as a wife, a writer, an abstract-thinking woman who dared to defy the authorities. Yet, deep down, I knew this was the right thing to do.

Now, back to my childhood. I was steeped in sorrow and suffering, brought about by my piety, and I was longing for redemption. This was my redemption: writing the books. Do you see? I followed the script, too, to create my own suffering at the end, the suffering that finally ended my life. I didn't need to. I just didn't know how to get past this kind of deep belief in the need for suffering, or any belief that goes so deeply into one's thinking.

This was coupled with my own inability to read between the lines sometimes. How willing would I be to capture the essence of the doctrine of Seth? It was for me doctrine. I followed the rules, you know, writing faithfully the messages of the gods. And I was able to capture a lot in those pages. But the reason I felt badly is because I was not really able to move past my own sense that I was causing harm to the Church. I wasn't fully capable of feeling that it would be okay. That's what ended my life eventually.

Therefore, I want to assure all of you that you will be okay, too. The necessary suffering of being in the world is the only suffering you will ever need to take on. The necessary sacrifices are the only ones you need to take on. You don't have to suffer endlessly nor make the total sacrifice of your lives. This will happen sometimes, yes, but they're not necessary for everybody.

The caution with which I proceeded, therefore, needs to be removed: you won't topple authoritarian systems overnight. This takes a lot of time, usually. But your small efforts make a difference. Don't let anyone tell you who to love or what to do with your lives. This might be the biggest change in your everyday lives that will eventually topple the worst kinds of systems.

My experiences in the nonphysical world were these. I woke up in my body. Even though I was dead, I was still feeling in my body. I had to be awakened, as I was sleeping. Those who woke me were angels which I had imagined, of course, in my Catholic doctrines that I'd learned as a girl. The angels escorted me from my body into a kind of sanitarium, the old kind where you went to recover. The place was very enjoyable.

There were doctors, nurses, and many kinds of other invalid types besides me who were caring and healing to be around.

I had to recover from the world of ideas a bit. As you know, perhaps, I was enthralled with ideas and wrote my own essay on the subject.[57] So the world of ideas was something I had with me without needing to start from scratch. The lessons of my life created the kind of structure I needed when moving from the physical world to the world of ideas itself.

This is where I am now, having been taken from the place of healing into the kind of state of being where I'm with many friends now, with Robbie, my cats, my home in Elmira. The very things I loved there are here, too. The seasons come and go. I paint the view from my window. I have a lot of friends around me. I can't tell you how grounded I feel now that I have realized the path from physical to nonphysical. The difference between me now and me then is simply this: I don't suffer anymore because I know it's not necessary, that's all.

The difference between myself and the self that I'm becoming is that I will not need to have my representations of my life as Jane around me all the

[57] In the fall of 1963, before Seth officially started speaking through her, Jane sat down at her kitchen table to write poetry. She remembered later, "It was very domestic, very normal, very unpsychedelic... Between one normal minute and the next, a fantastic avalanche of radical, new ideas burst into my head with tremendous force ... It was as if the physical world were really tissue-paper-thin, hiding infinite dimensions of reality, and I was flung through the tissue paper with a huge ripping sound." She wrote furiously during this trance state and eventually published it as *The Physical Universe as Idea Construction*.

time. Without them, without the memories, I will go into new spaces in which I'm welcomed as a colleague. Now, you will notice that I'm there now, too, part of this Committee of authors. I don't need to think about being here or there, I'm all of that, even as I was when physical, the way you are now, too. The path will differentiate without needing to be fully <u>there</u>, or <u>there</u>, or <u>there</u>.

Do you see? You're here now, too, with me. You're in the bigger space with your friends here, too. You're with your very best friends now!

With the writing of this book, we've been able to share with you the glorious afterlife that awaits you without your needing to feel afraid at all. What better gift to allow yourselves to understand what really is true? If not, we will make sure you do when you see us here, in the beautiful afterlife.

We want to express our deepest gratitude for hearing us. We want to assure you that we will be with you in your dreams as much as you'd like us to.

Dream on, dear humans. Dream on.

With loving thoughts,

Jane Roberts

ABOUT THE AUTHOR

Joanne Helfrich is an author and channeler whose works promote personal and collective transformation (*joannehelfrich.com*). She is a cofounder and principal instructor at NewWorldView (*newworldview.com*), a provider of educational programs that explore the practical applications of conscious creation—how we create our own reality. With the essence of Rose, she provides private sessions to help individuals embrace their soul's design for deepest fulfillment (*thewayofspirit.com*). She lives in Topanga, California, with her husband and collaborator, Paul M. Helfrich.

Other books by Joanne Helfrich

The Way of Spirit:
Teachings of Rose

The Afterlife of J.D. Salinger:
A Beautiful Message from Beyond

Let That Shit Go:
Learn to Process Loss and Be Happy

Made in United States
North Haven, CT
03 May 2022

18835402R00146